THE NEW JERSEY FAMILY LAW HANDBOOK

A REFERENCE GUIDE TO NEW JERSEY CASE LAW AND STATUTES GOVERNING:

Marriage
Children & adoption
Parentage
Divorce & alimony
Custody & child support

John M. B. Balouziyeh, JD

THE NEW JERSEY FAMILY LAW HANDBOOK
A Reference Guide to New Jersey Case Law and Statutes

ISBN (13): 978-0-9845182-1-0
ISBN (10): 0-9845182-1-0

JuraLaw

Published by JURALAW™
an imprint of TELLERBOOKS™

t TellerBooks

TABLE OF CONTENTS

ABBREVIATIONS

CAPTA................... Child Abuse Prevention and Treatment Act
DOMA .... Defense of Marriage Act
DPA....................... Domestic Partnership Act
DYFS .... Division of Youth and Family Services
FACTS................... Family Automated Case Tracking System
N.J. Rev. Stat. .... New Jersey Revised Statutes
NJTF .... New Jersey Task Force on Child Abuse and Neglect Act
PKPA..................... Parental Kidnapping Prevention Act
PDVA .... Prevention of Domestic Violence Act of 1991
UCCJA .... Uniform Child Custody Jurisdiction Act
UCCJEA................ Uniform Child Custody Jurisdiction and Enforcement Act
UPAA.................... Uniform Premarital Agreement Act
VAWA .... Violence Against Women Act of 2000

for
Alexa
and the One who makes all things possible

PREFACE

I am pleased to present *The New Jersey Family Law Handbook* to New Jersey residents and others who may have an interest— professional, academic, or otherwise—in navigating New Jersey's legal provisions as they relate to the family.

This *Handbook* is comprehensive and thorough while providing clarity to lawyers and non-lawyers alike. It takes a methodical approach towards explaining the various sections of the New Jersey Code relating to the family, marriage, divorce, children, and parentage, while exploring how these statutes have interacted with the New Jersey and federal Constitutions. The *Handbook* aptly discusses key decisions of the United States and New Jersey Supreme Courts, from *Maynard v. Hill* (U.S.) defining marriage in 1888 to *Lewis v. Harris* (N.J.) deciding on same-sex marriage in New Jersey in 2006, and how these decisions shape the family in New Jersey today.

This book does not discuss ideas in the abstract only; it also delves into the practical issues that affect New Jersey families and others with ties to the state. It goes into questions of when a marriage is valid, how the application for a restraining order may be filed, where the adoption process begins, and many others pertaining to prenuptial agreements, marital dissolution, alimony and child support payments, and so forth.

I am confidant that this book will be a valuable resource to New Jersey residents seeking to exercise their legal rights and better familiarize themselves with the procedures involved therein. It will also serve as an important guide to attorneys seeking an overview of New Jersey family law. The *Handbook's* meticulous citations allow readers to easily find primary sources in order to delve into further research. Also included are useful excerpts of the major New Jersey family law regulations, such as the Uniform Premarital Agreement Act and the Child Abuse Prevention and Treatment Act.

Well-structured, clearly organized, and easy to navigate, this *Handbook* is a must-have on the bookshelf of any person involved in a New Jersey family law matter.

- Lynne Marie Kohm
  John Brown McCarty Professor of Family Law
  Regent University School of Law

1.

INTRODUCTION

Family law occupies a position of special importance in American society. Legal questions pertaining to family law are among the most debated in academia, politics, and the media. Political candidates often center their campaigns on critical family law questions, such as whether there is a right of women to choose an abortion or of same-sex couples to marry.

Family law, perhaps more than any other area of the law, affects our daily lives in many ways. Whether it is marriage and prenuptial agreements, the family and parentage, children, adoption, or assisted reproductive technology, almost all of us will in some way come into contact with family law.

This book provides a framework that facilitates a clear understanding of New Jersey family law. It will help New Jersey residents to more effectively use the services of attorneys and other professionals with whom they may consult in order to better understand or exercise their legal rights.

WHY A BOOK ON NEW JERSEY FAMILY LAW?

While publications laying out the legal framework of the family exist in other states, such texts in New Jersey are limited to scholarly treatises designed for academics or legal practitioners. No book lays out New Jersey family law in a clear, concise text that is easily accessible to the non-lawyer.

This book now fills that void, providing New Jersey residents with a clear, concise summary of New Jersey family law. The main objective of this book is to serve the people of New Jersey by building their confidence in navigating and understanding the New Jersey legal system to make informed decisions. This book seeks to supply information on the state of the law in New Jersey and on the rights of New Jerseyans and to provide a reliable overview of the leading cases and principal statutes that shape New Jersey family law. Although this book cannot replace legal advice tailored to individual needs, it will enable readers to enter legal consultations with more knowledge and familiarity of their legal options and thus more confidence. It may also show readers when they may resolve conflicts on their own and when they should hire an attorney.

This book will further help students and practitioners as a quick reference on a particular point of law or as a starting point for further research.

THE N.J. FAMILY COURT SYSTEM

Basic Structure of the New Jersey Court System

Any person involved in a family law matter will likely come to use the courts of the State of New Jersey, and will thus be well served by a basic understanding of the structure and hierarchy of the New Jersey judicial system.

The courts of New Jersey, as provided by the New Jersey Constitution,[1] are divided into three classes:

- *The New Jersey Supreme Court.* Formerly the "Court of Errors and Appeals," this is the highest appeals court in the state;
- *The New Jersey Superior Court.* This is a statewide court with appellate jurisdiction (Appellate Division) and trial jurisdiction (Law and Chancery Divisions). It was formerly comprised of the "Supreme Court," "Court of Chancery," and "Prerogative Court";
- *Various lower courts.* These courts hold limited jurisdiction and include county and municipal courts and tax courts.

---

[1] N.J. Const. art. VI, § I.

The New Jersey Superior Court is governed by article VI, § III of the New Jersey Constitution. The court exercises its trial and appeals jurisdiction through three Divisions:

- *Appellate Division.* With its eight parts (A through H), it hears appeals from the Law and Chancery Divisions, as well as from administrative agencies.
- *Law Division.* This is the trial court in law, and is divided into a Civil Part, which hears claims with no monetary limit on the value of claims heard, and a Special Civil Part, which in turn has a Landlord/Tenant section, a regular Special Civil section hearing claims of $3,000 - $15,000, and a Small Claims section hearing claims for up to $3,000 or $5,000 if a tenant is demanding the return of a security deposit;
- *Chancery Division.* This is the trial court in equity, and is divided into three parts: (i) the *General Equity Part*, handling cases where equity is primarily sought; (ii) the *Probate Part* handling probate matters, guardianship, and related matters; and (iii) the *Family Part*, handling all family-related matters.

Family Part of the Chancery Division

With over 350,000 cases heard every year,[2] the Family Part deals with marriage and domestic relations, divorce, child support, custody and visitation, termination of parental rights, foster-care placements, adoption, juvenile matters, and domestic violence.

The Family Part replaced the juvenile and domestic relations courts. Judges in the Family Part may hold office for seven years and, if reappointed, may obtain life tenure.[3]

---

[2] New Jersey Judiciary, Family Practice Division, available at
<http://www.judiciary.state.nj.us/family/index.htm>.
[3] N.J. Const., art. VI, § VI.

FAMILY PRACTICE DIVISION

Overview

The Family Practice Division is part of the Trial Court Services Division of the Administrative Office of the Courts. It implements policy, analyzes best practices, and seeks input from citizens and volunteers on the efficacy of the N.J. Family Division of the court system. This section discusses some of the programs of the Family Practice Division that have as their goal the amelioration of services provided to New Jersey residents within the context of the administration of family law.

Programs

The Family Practice Division has a statistical unit, which uses a data system called "FACTS" (*Family Automated Case Tracking System*). This system is used to monitor best practices compliance, improve case processing, and evaluate court programs. For example, if a new resident to New Jersey comes from a state that granted a restraining order in his or her favor, FACTS can record the restraining order in New Jersey in order to enforce it and thus grant full faith and credit to the original order.

Another program maintained by the Family Practice Division is the *Child Support Hearing Officer Program*, through which a Child Support Officer hears cases concerning child support and offers an expedited alternative to court proceedings. The officer's recommendation is signed by a judge and has the force of a court order. However, parties who disagree with the Officer's decision may have the matter heard by a judge.

Over 10,000 juvenile delinquency cases are heard each year in New Jersey, not by the courts, but by *Juvenile Conference Committees*.[4] Each committee consists of six to nine volunteers who hear cases of delinquency throughout New Jersey whenever minors

---

[4] New Jersey Judiciary, Family Division (Overview), available at <http://www.judiciary.state.nj.us/family/fam-07.htm>.

are involved. The Family Practice Division provides a guide and trains Juvenile Conference Committee volunteers.

Among its *other services*, the Family Practice Division provides the New Jersey Legislature with information on the implementation of new laws that benefit and protect the family and makes recommendations to the Supreme Court regarding the rules that affect the practice of family law in New Jersey.[5]

NOTE ON SOURCES

This *Handbook* draws primarily from the New Jersey Revised Statutes, with particular attention given to:

- Title 2A, Subtitle 6A: Abortion and Sterilization;
- Title 9: Children – Juvenile and Domestic Relations Courts;
- Title 26, Chapter 8A: Domestic Partnerships;
- Title 30, Subtitle 1A: Division of Family Development;
- Title 37: Marriage and Married Persons; and
- Title 54A: New Jersey Gross Income Tax, Chapter 3. Personal Exemptions and Deductions (alimony, separate maintenance, etc.).

Attention is also given Appendix IX-A of the Rules Governing the Courts of the State of New Jersey, which lays out the guidelines to be used for child support determinations.

This guide provides a brief summary of statutes that in their original form span several hundred pages. The major state and federal cases interpreting these statutes and commenting on their constitutionality are also discussed herein.

Because of the expansive breadth its topics, this book will review main ideas, but will not touch on every point. Readers wishing to go further are encouraged to consult the Table of Authorities in order to find full case citations in order to access the cases directly. Most of these cases, and particularly those of the New Jersey and United States Supreme Courts, are published online.

---

[5] *Id.*

Readers may also wish to consult excerpts from the relevant statutes reprinted in the appendices at the end of this volume. The statutes in their entirety are also available at many local libraries and at any law library, particularly those of a local law school.

Yet reading statutes without a guide may be a daunting task, and consulting them without annotations can be misleading, since some expired laws continue to appear on the books. To avoid misunderstanding, the reader may wish to acquire an annotated copy of the New Jersey Statutes. Mark Guralnick's *New Jersey Family Law Annotated*, published by Thompson West, is a leading text in this respect, and is frequently updated.

2.

MARRIAGE

In *Maynard v. Hill*, the U.S. Supreme Court defined marriage as "something more than a mere contract, though founded upon the agreement of the parties." The rights and obligations of marriage depend "not upon their agreement, but upon the law."[6] Marriage is thus a societal institution regulated and controlled by public authority. Because it is not a mere contract, legislation may affect the institution and even annul the relation between the parties without violated the U.S. Constitution.

In this chapter, we will examine the regulations of the institution of marriage, as provided by the New Jersey law under the confines of the U.S. Constitution.

REQUIREMENTS FOR ENTRY INTO MARRIAGE

Age and Consent

In order to enter into marriage, both parties must be eighteen years of age or older. Otherwise, the consent of the parents is necessary. If the minor is under sixteen years of age, the consent of a judge in addition to the consent of the parents is necessary. The judge's approval must be delivered to the licensing officer.

The consent of the parents or judge is not required for a male under eighteen years of age if: (i) the male has been arrested for having sexual intercourse with a woman of good repute for sexual

---

[6] *Maynard v. Hill*, 125 U.S. 190 (1888).

chastity; (ii) the woman has become pregnant; and (iii) he applies for a marriage license.[7]

Prohibited Degrees of Familial Relation

Furthermore, the parties may not be within prohibited degrees of familial relation. Specifically, an individual may not marry an ancestor, descendent, brother or sister, aunt or uncle, or niece or nephew.[8] New Jersey does, however, permit marriage between cousins, whether first cousins or cousins more distantly related (second cousins, first cousins once removed, etc.). In this respect, New Jersey is like nineteen other states.

Bigamy/Polygamy

At the time of marriage, neither party may already be married. If a party was at one time married, a divorce or annulment must be registered with the relevant civil authorities, either in New Jersey or elsewhere.

Competence/Venereal Disease

Each party must be neither mentally incompetent nor have any venereal disease in a communicable stage.[9] The New Jersey Statutes provide that the person issuing marriage licenses "shall make information available to applicants concerning places where such applicants may be tested for genetic diseases,"[10] yet it does not state that applicants are required to undergo such testing. Furthermore, there appears to be little evidence that municipalities issuing marriage licenses enforce the prohibition on applicants with venereal diseases in a communicable stage from marrying or that such applicants are penalized for contracting marriage. Applications for marriage licenses in New Jersey required applicants to attest as to whether they carried such diseases as of

---

[7] N.J. Rev. Stat. § 37:1-6.

[8] *Id.* § 37:1-1.

[9] *Id.* § 37:1-9.

[10] *Id.* § 37:1-27.

2002, but in the revised form used at the time of writing,[11] no reference is made to venereal diseases. Furthermore, applicants are not required to undergo blood tests in order to marry in New Jersey.

Ceremony

The marriage must be solemnized by a person, institution, religious society, or organization authorized by the New Jersey code. State law authorizes New Jersey federal and state judges, state clerks, mayors, deputy mayors, chairs of New Jersey township committees, and religious ministers to solemnize marriages.[12] If the parties fail to meet this element, their marriage will be held absolutely void.[13]

Obtaining and Delivering the Marriage License

The parties being married must obtain a marriage license from the municipality in which the ceremony will be performed and deliver it to the person or religious society or institution that will solemnize the marriage.[14] There is generally a seventy two-hour waiting period between when the parties apply for the marriage license, and when it is issued. The marriage license is valid for thirty days from the date of issuance.[15]

Failure of the parties to apply for and obtain a valid marriage license renders the marriage absolutely void,[16] unless the marriage was entered into before December 1, 1939, when common law marriages were permitted.[17]

---

[11] Form REG-77, FEB 07, is used as of 2010.
[12] N.J. Rev. Stat. § 37:1-13.
[13] *Id.* § 37:1-10.
[14] *Id.* § 37:1-2.
[15] *Id.* § 37:1-4.
[16] *Id.* § 37:1-10.
[17] *See infra.*, "Common Law Marriage," for more detailed treatment.

COMMON LAW MARRIAGES

As previously discussed, in order to obtain the rights and responsibilities of marriage, couples must obtain a marriage license and deliver it to the person or society officiating the ceremony. However, marriages entered into before December 1, 1939 are granted an exception to this rule. Such marriages are legally recognized as common law marriages even if the parties failed to obtain a marriage license.[18]

To qualify for marriage under the common law, the parties must: (i) be in agreement to put themselves out as husband and wife; (ii) actually put themselves out as married while having capacity to marry; and (iii) be in an exclusive relationship.

For all marriages contracted after December 1, 1939, a marriage license is required in order for the marriage to be recognized as such under the state law. There is an exception for the common law marriages of other states, which New Jersey recognizes when the common law requirements of the respective state were met by the couple while they were living in that state.

ANNULMENTS

Introduction

Like divorce, annulment voids the validity of marriage. However, unlike divorce, which voids the validity of a marriage already in existence, annulment treats a marriage as though it never occurred or existed. When a marriage is annulled, it is considered to never have had any validity from its beginning.

In order to obtain an annulment, the marriage must either be void or voidable.

Void Marriage

A void marriage[19] is one that is prohibited by public policy and the law. Thus, the annulment of void marriage applies only when there

---

[18] N.J. Rev. Stat. § 37:1-10.
[19] N.J. Rev. Stat. § 2A:34-1.

is a defect in the marriage so serious as to render the marriage void as against public policy. Nothing that either party can do will have the effect of validating the marriage. Examples of void marriages include the following:

-   *Bigamous marriages*, in which one spouse was married at the time of the second marriage; and
-   *Marriages between related parties* (*i.e.*, marriage with an ancestor, descendent, sibling, aunt or uncle, or niece or nephew). The validity of a marriage between related parties will not, however, be questioned after the death of either spouse if, during the lifetime of the spouses, the marriage was not annulled.

In order to obtain an annulment of a void marriage, the party seeking the annulment must prove that circumstances from before the marriage was contracted rendered it invalid. No proceeding is necessary to obtain the annulment.

Voidable Marriage

Voidable marriage,[20] on the other hand, is not illegal by default. It may become valid through the ratification of the parties and may only become void through a court proceeding.

Examples of voidable marriages include those where the parties did not intend to get married (*lack of intent*) and marriages where either party lacked capacity to enter into the marriage because of a mental condition or drug use (*incapacity*). Marriages in which **assent was obtained by improper means**, such as through duress, undue influence, or fraud, may also be voided. In addition, when either spouse was **under the age of eighteen** at the time of the marriage, and he or she has not ratified or confirmed the marriage upon reaching the age of eighteen, the marriage may be voided. Finally, a marriage may be voided when one spouse suffers from **sterility** or **impotence** and the party seeking annulment was ignorant of this when entering into the marriage. The sterility or

---

[20] *Id.*

impotence must be incurable and the party seeking annulment must not have subsequently ratified the marriage.

Procedure

Annulment is permitted under the equity jurisdiction of the Superior Court.[21] As with divorce, annulment will not be granted unless one or both spouses were New Jersey residents for at least one year.

DOMESTIC PARTNERSHIPS

The New Jersey Legislature, resolving to support domestic partnerships of both same sex and opposite sex unmarried cohabitants, passed the Domestic Partnership Act (DPA), which took effect on July 10, 2004.[22] The Legislature passed the Act pursuant to its conclusions that domestic partnerships support the "financial, physical, and emotional health of their participants."[23]

The benefits afforded to unmarried cohabitants include the following:

- Protection against all forms of discrimination against unmarried cohabitants;
- Health benefits, including hospital visitation rights and the right to make decisions for an incapacitated domestic partner;
- Tax benefits, including additional exemption from personal income tax and transfer inheritance tax that are treated as though the cohabitants were married; and
- Certain health and pension benefits (afforded only to same-sex cohabitants, since they may not enter into and enjoy the benefits of marriage).[24]

---

[21] *Id.* § 2A:34-1.f.
[22] NJ Taxation, The Domestic Partnership Act, available at <http://www.state.nj.us/treasury/taxation/index.html?dompartact.htm~mainFrame>.
[23] N.J. Rev. Stat. § 26:8A-2.b.
[24] *Id.* § 26:8A-2.d-e.

The division of property of unmarried living partners is treated differently by different states when the partners stop living together.

The *majority view* denied unmarried cohabitants the same rights of married couples and prefers instead to delegate this to legislatures as a policy decision. For example, in *Hewitt v. Hewitt*,[25] the court denied the plaintiff the right to half of the defendant's property, even after the parties lived together for fifteen years and raised three children together, because they were not married.

New Jersey, on the other hand, accepts the *minority approach*, which recognizes as enforceable for the purpose of dividing property both express contracts as well as contracts implied through conduct. This approach was demonstrated in the case *Marvin v. Marvin*,[26] where the plaintiff argued that she exchanged her services as companion, homemaker, housekeeper, and cook for the defendant's support. She claimed that she therefore had an implied contract with the defendant for half of the property collected during the years when they were living together as unmarried cohabitants. The court agreed.

SAME-SEX MARRIAGE

In New Jersey

Traditionally, marriage in New Jersey could only be entered into between one man and one woman *Rothman v. Rothman*.[27] However, in October of 2006, in the controversial decision in *Lewis v. Harris*,[28] the New Jersey Supreme Court held that equal protection requires all of the benefits of marriage to be extended to same-sex couples.

In a four-three opinion, the court declared that, although there is no fundamental right to gay marriage in the New Jersey Constitution or otherwise, the New Jersey Legislature was required to create a structure through which committed gay couples could

---

[25] *Hewit v. Hewitt*, 394 N.E. 2d 1204 (Il. 1979).
[26] *Marvin v. Marvin*, 557 P.2d 106 (Ca. 1976).
[27] *Rothman v. Rothman*, 65 N.J. 219, 320 A.2d 496 (N.J. 1974).
[28] *Lewis v. Harris*, 2006 N.J. Lexis 1521 (N.J. 2006).

receive all of the benefits of marriage. The Court unanimously held that gay couples had the same rights as heterosexual married partners, and that "denying rights and benefits to committed same-sex couples that are statutorily given to their heterosexual counterparts violates the equal protection guarantee of article I, Paragraph 1" of the New Jersey Constitution.[29]

The majority conceded that the framers of the New Jersey Constitution and the drafters of the marriage statutes "could not have imagined that the liberty right protected by [the state Constitution] embraced the right of a person to marry someone of his or her own sex" and that the historical understanding of marriage, an understanding "as old as the book Genesis," recognized marriage as an institution between one man and one woman.[30] Dismissing these originalist arguments, the Court went on to affirm that "[t]imes and attitudes have changed"[31] and that New Jersey jurisprudence should reflect these new times and attitudes by prohibiting any "differential treatment based on sexual orientation."[32]

The New Jersey Legislature was therefore required to either: (i) amend marriage statutes in order to grant gay couples the same rights as married couples; or (ii) "enact a statutory structure" to provide for the all of the benefits of marriage to same-sex partners.[33] There was one third option that the Supreme Court never mentioned: the Legislature's right to amend the Constitution in order to ban same-sex marriage. If the Legislature had chosen this third course, it would have effectively voided the Court's decision and any later decision entitling same-sex partners to the benefits of marriage.

Acting with due speed, the Legislature adopted the second option that the Court prescribed. On December 14, 2006, the Legislature passed a bill legalizing same-sex civil unions that

---

[29] *Id.* 18.
[30] *Id.* 45.
[31] *Id.*
[32] *Id.* 46.
[33] *Id.* 19.

extend the benefits of marriage to same-sex partners.[34] Although the new law does not refer to the same-sex unions as "marriage," same-sex partners enjoy all of the benefits of marriage.

The bill surprised many because of its unusual haste, having been passed just fifty days after the Court handed down the decision giving the Legislature 180 days to choose its course of action.[35] The speed with which the bill was passed into law was even more surprising in light of highly divided public opinion over gay marriage and civil unions.[36] By passing the law, the Legislature effectively eschewed calls by many conservatives to ban gay marriage and civil unions by amending the New Jersey Constitution.[37]

Measures Adopted in Other States

New Jersey has become the third state to recognize same-sex civil unions, rejecting the approach of the majority of states, which have enacted some form of the federal Defense of Marriage Act (DOMA), which defines marriage as between one man and one woman and allows states to refuse to recognize same-sex marriage deemed constitutional in other states. As of 2004, some thirty eight states have passed state DOMAs that deny recognition of gay marriages entered into in other states without ever making reference to the

---

[34] Laura Mansnerus, "Legislators Vote for Gay Unions in New Jersey" (New York Times, Dec. 15, 2006).

[35] *Lewis v. Harris*, 94.

[36] *See, e.g.*, "New Jersey Voters Divided Over Same-Sex Marriage" (Rutgers-Eagleton Poll, October 25, 2006), p. 1 (showing an electorate nearly equally divided on the question of same-sex marriage, with 44% opposing it as of June 2006), available at <http://eagletonpoll.rutgers.edu/polls/EagletonPoll_GayMarriageData.pdf>.

[37] *See, e.g.* Alliance Defense Fund, "New Jersey Supreme Court Denies Victory to Same-Sex 'Marriage' Advocates, But Need for Marriage Amendments Reaffirmed..." (Alliance Defense Fund, Oct. 25, 2006) (calling for the passing of an amendment banning same-sex marriage), available at <http://www.alliancedefensefund.org/userdocs/updates/special/2006_1025.html>.

federal law.[38] New Jersey also stands out against many other states that have adopted constitutional amendments limiting marriage to heterosexual couples.[39]

Twenty seven states have also passed amendments defining marriage as a union between one man and one woman. Arizona proposed one such Amendment, but it failed to succeed. In those states where the amendments passed, legislation recognizing same-sex marriage is effectively banned. Some of these statutes also place a ban on civil unions.

Homosexual groups and rights advocates have had difficulty in mobilizing communities to oppose marriage amendments that ban same-sex marriage. However, in opposing amendments that ban both same-sex marriage as well as civil unions, they have been able to garner the support of heterosexual groups that support civil unions and wish to see them legislatively recognized. A strategy of many homosexual advocate groups has thus been to rally communities in defeating this second category of marriage amendments.[40]

New Jersey has neither a constitutional amendment nor a proposal for a constitutional amendment banning gay marriage.

---

[38] Jason Manning, "The Defense of Marriage Act" (PBS Online NewsHour, Apr. 30, 2004), available at
<http://www.pbs.org/newshour/bb/law/gay_marriage/act.html>.
[39] Associated Press, "Voters pass all 11 bans on gay marriage" (MSNBC, Nov. 3, 2004) (showing that all of the states with constitutional amendments banning same-sex marriage on their ballots passed the ballots).
[40] William C. Duncan, "Friends with Benefits?" *National Review Online*, available at < http://www.nationalreview.com/articles/218909/friends-benefits/william-c-duncan>.

3.

MARITAL CONTRACTS

INTRODUCTION

The term "marital contract" refers to the broad umbrella of agreements entered into between former, present, or future spouses. Marital contracts deal with property division, alimony (spousal support), living expenses, and other issues in light of divorce, separation, as well as reconciliation. They can also anticipate events and provide solutions to hardships that may arise during the course of marriage.

There are many types of marital contracts and agreements, including property settlement agreements, ante-nuptial agreements, reconciliation agreements (for couples that have separated and hope to become reconciled), and cohabitation agreements.

PREMARITAL AGREEMENTS

When entered into before marriage, marital contracts are referred to as "antenuptial agreements," "premarital agreements," "premarital contracts," "prenuptial agreements," or simply, "prenups." A premarital agreement[41] is thus an agreement entered into prior to marriage that deals with alimony (spousal support), property division, and other issues that may arise if the marriage is dissolved or if one of the spouses dies.[42]

---

[41] N.J. Rev. Stat. §§ 37:2-31-41.
[42] *Black's Law Dictionary* 1220 "prenuptial agreement" (Bryan A. Garner ed., 8th ed., West 2004).

The agreement may also discuss any other issues that the parties wish to have settled prior to contracting marriage, including the payment of expenses during the marriage; the rights to buy, sell, control, and manage property; the disposition of property and payment of alimony upon separation or divorce; the distribution of property in the event of death; or the freedom to pursue careers. Premarital agreements will generally be enforced, unless they encourage divorce.

Upon the marriage of the parties, the agreement becomes effective, but it may be revoked at any time by a writing signed by both parties, with or without consideration.

Under the **Uniform Premarital Agreement Act** (UPAA), which New Jersey has adopted, the premarital agreement itself similarly does not require consideration in order to be valid. However, the agreement must meet the following elements:

- It must be in **writing** (under the statute of frauds);
- With a **disclosure** of assets; and
- **Signed** by both parties.[43]

In *Gilbert v. Gilbert*,[44] the court refused to enforce the defendant husband's promise to grant the plaintiff wife certain property in consideration of her marrying him, since his promise was not in writing. The rule in equity removing contracts from the statute of frauds whenever one party partially performs was held inapplicable to ante-nuptial agreements, as in this case.

All of the elements of contractual defenses apply to marital contracts, including unconscionability, undue influence, duress, and fraud. Thus, as in all other contracts, assent to a premarital agreement must be **voluntary** and can be set aside if a party can show that it was not voluntary. In addition, it may be set aside if one of the spouses: (i) did not fully disclose financial assets; (ii) did not waive any right of disclosure of the property; (iii) did not have or could not have adequate knowledge of the property of his or her

---

[43] N.J. Rev. Stat. § 37:2-33.
[44] *Gilbert v. Gilbert*, 66 N.J. Super. 246 (App. Div. 1961).

spouse; (iv) did not consult with legal counsel and did not waive that right.

POSTNUPTIAL AGREEMENTS, MARRIAGE SETTLEMENTS

Marital contracts are referred to as "postnuptial agreements," "postnuptial settlements," or simply as "postnups," when entered into after marriage is contracted and no divorce, separation, or marital dissolution is imminent. Postnuptial agreements deal with issues of property division and support.[45]

On the contrary, when such an agreement is entered into after marriage in anticipation of divorce, the agreement is referred to as a "property settlement," "marriage settlement," or "marital agreement."[46]

COVENANT MARRIAGE CONTRACTS

A covenant marriage is a marriage where the spouses agree to more stringent standards for entering into marriage and obtaining a divorce than those required by state law. Generally, this means that the couple may not (i) marry without premarital counseling; nor (ii) divorce without marital counseling and separate living arrangements for a determined period of time. However, the requirement of marital counseling and separate living arrangements may be waived if one spouse is at fault, due to, for example, adultery, abuse, or abandonment.[47]

New Jersey has no statute recognizing covenant marriage. Yet this does not impede the parties from opting for this form, as long as the terms of such marriage are laid out in a validly formed contract that does not contravene New Jersey public policy.

---

[45] *Black's Law Dictionary* 1206 "postnuptial agreement" (8th ed. 2004).
[46] *Id.*
[47] *Black's Law Dictionary* 993 "covenant marriage" (8th ed. 2004).

4.

MARITAL DISSOLUTION

MARRIAGE AND DIVORCE AS FUNDAMENTAL RIGHTS

The U.S. Supreme Court has held on a number of occasions that access to marriage is a fundamental right in a high position on the hierarchy of socially valued institutions. The state may not unreasonably limit access to marriage or access to divorce in its courts. This includes a prohibition on limiting access to state courts to indigent individuals seeking marriage or divorce on the basis of their inability to pay filing fees. Such impediments would violate the due process rights of such individuals.

This rule was established in *Boddie v. Connecticut*,[48] where welfare recipients challenged a District Court that held that the state was permitted to impose fees that could impede the indigent from seeking divorce. The U.S. Supreme Court held that because the state monopolizes society's access to marriage and divorce, both of which are important social institutions, it must not impose fees that limit individuals' access to either one. Doing so would violate the Constitution, as it would limit the due process rights of indigent individuals by depriving them of the opportunity to be heard. The District Court judgment was reversed.

SEPARATION

Separation in New Jersey refers to the situation in which a married couple lives apart. There is no formal judicial proceeding for separation in New Jersey; the parties simply choose to live apart. If,

---

[48] *Boddie v. Connecticut*, 401 U.S. 371 (1971).

on the other hand, one of the parties decides to file for a no-fault divorce, he or she may do so by filing for divorce in the relevant court if the period of separation has been eighteen months or more.

Outside of the court system and litigation, the parties may independently come to agreements regarding their expenses during the separation. The parties may also through a judicial proceeding obtain court orders determining payments of *separate maintenance* (money paid by one spouse to support the other when the couple is no longer living together as husband and wife) as well as temporary child support and child custody.

The parties come to agree on various issues, including living expenses, support, and property division, by means of a *separation agreement* that is drafted and implemented outside of the court system. The separation agreement, like a premarital agreement, may look towards divorce or, like a reconciliation agreement, may be focused on reconciling the spouses while providing for living expenses and other practical concerns while they are living apart.

The separation agreement that the parties draft will almost always be enforced. When the parties are able to come to an agreement regarding support and custody, the agreement will usually serve as the basis for the divorce judgment if the parties later file for divorce, provided the agreement is fair and freely entered into.

However, a separation agreement, like a marital contract, can be set aside for fraud, unconscionability, undue influence, or duress. In addition, courts will set aside separation agreements when there is mutual mistake or changed circumstances or if one of the spouses was unable to have the agreement reviewed by counsel and did not waive the right to do so.

A spouse will not be required to offer support to the other if he or she can prove, for example, that the other spouse engaged in adultery, as adultery justifies withholding support. The spouse's commission of a matrimonial offense is a defense against the requirement for paying separate maintenance.[49]

DIVORCE FROM BED AND BOARD

Divorce from bed and board[50] has characteristics of both separation as well as divorce from the bonds of matrimony. Like full divorce from the bonds of matrimony, the parties are economically divorced, with alimony and the other financial consequences of divorce in force.[51] Unlike divorce, however, the parties remain legally married. Divorce from bed and board is thus like separation, but with a judicial decree, and is referred to by some courts as "judicial separation" or "legal separation." The requirements and procedures for obtaining a divorce from bed and board are the same as those for a divorce from the bonds of matrimony.

Once the divorce from bed and board is granted, the parties may pursue several different courses. If they later reconcile, they may petition the court for a revocation or suspension of the judgment for a divorce from bed and board. If, on the other hand, they seek to fully dissolve the bonds of marriage, they may apply for a judgment for divorce from the bonds of matrimony. This will allow each party to then remarry, which would otherwise be legally impossible without a court order pronouncing full divorce from the bonds of matrimony.

DIVORCE FROM THE BONDS OF MATRIMONY

General Requirements

Divorce from the bonds of matrimony is the New Jersey equivalent of no-fault divorce, where one spouse is able to obtain a divorce order on the grounds that the other spouse committed some wrong against the marriage (adultery, extreme cruelty, abandonment, etc.). Like no-fault divorce, which is described below, it requires one

---

[49] *Sabbarese v. Sabbarese*, 104 N.J. Eq. 600 (Ch. 1929).
[50] N.J. Rev. Stat. § 2A:34-3.
[51] *Id.* § 2A:34-6.

party to have been a state resident for at least one year at the time that the divorce proceedings begin. One exception to this rule is divorce based on adultery, where a party may file regardless of how long she has been a resident, as long as she was a resident from the time she discovered the adultery to the time the divorce action began.

After the divorce proceedings begin, they may proceed even if both parties leave New Jersey thereafter.

Fault Grounds for Divorce

Divorce from the bonds of matrimony, unlike no-fault divorce, requires the party seeking the divorce to show some statutorily-defined fault attributable to his spouse. The grounds for divorce are laid out in N.J. Rev. Stat. § 2A:34-2.

Extreme Cruelty

This cause of action may involve either physical or mental abuse that endangers the plaintiff's health or safety. The abuse need not be repeated. In *Kram v. Kram*,[52] the court defined extreme cruelty as the degree of cruelty that in the present or past threatens the life or health of the aggrieved party or causes such discomfort and wretchedness as to incapacitate her from discharging her marital duties. An example that would qualify is marital rape. However, because the court applies a subjective standard taking into account the state of mind of the aggrieved party, what may appear to be frivolous to an outside observer may become a valid ground for divorce.

A spouse may not file a complaint for divorce based on extreme cruelty until a waiting period of three months since the last incident of abuse reported in the complaint has passed.

Adultery

Adultery is defined as the voluntary rejection of one's spouse and entry into an intimate relationship with any other party, regardless

---

[52] *Kram v. Kram*, 94 N.J. Super. 539 (Ch. Div. 1967).

of the gender and marital status of the third party, and regardless of whether sexual intercourse was consummated with the third party.[53] Raping a woman other than a man's wife also constitutes adultery for the purpose of divorce.[54] There is *no waiting period* required, and the one year residency requirement is waived, provided the victim spouse was living in New Jersey from the moment she discovered the adultery to the moment she files for divorce.

To prove adultery, it is not necessary to offer the testimony of an eye-witness stating that the parties engaged in sexual conduct or other evidence proving the same. Rather, adultery will be presumed whenever *opportunity* and *inclination* are proven. To prove opportunity, it must be shown that the adulterous spouse and a third party were in a private place where they would be able to engage in sexual relations if they so desired. To prove inclination, it must be shown that the couple was together, demonstrated affection or close physical contact, including embracing, kissing, or holding hands.[55]

Other ways of proving adultery include DNA tests of children born of the illicit lover and hotel records of the guilty spouse with her lover. Finally, admissions of the alleged adulterer serve as evidence. Historically, such an admission was *banned because of the possibility of collusion.* Today, however, a judge would likely use such evidence in an adultery hearing, since there is little incentive to collude given the availability of no-fault divorce.

According to N.J. Court Rule 5:7-3, New Jersey no longer requires *corroborating evidence* for establishing the elements of any fault-based divorce or annulment, including divorce based on adultery.[56]

If the plaintiff successfully proves adultery, he will be granted the divorce, unless the defendant successfully invokes a defense. Traditionally, collusion, recrimination, condonation, and the clean

---

[53] *S.B. v. S.J.B.*, 609 A.2d 124 (N.J. Super. Ct. 1992).
[54] *Johnson v. Johnson*, 80 A. 119 (N.J. Ch. 1911).
[55] *Atha v. Atha*, 121 A. 301 (N.J. Ch. 1923).
[56] *Kinsella v. Kinsella*, 696 A.2d 556 (N.J. 1997).

hands doctrine all served as defenses in divorce cases based on adultery. However, all have been abolished by statute with the exception of collusion (*see infra.*, "Defenses to Divorce," for more detailed treatment), and even collusion is not used by some New Jersey courts as a defense.

Abandonment (Desertion)

This defense may be invoked when the abandonment is willful and continuous for a period of at least twelve months. Abandonment is proved with evidence showing that the parties have been living separate and apart. Defenses historically raised for abandonment include *provocation* and *condonation*. Although provocation still exists as a defense in the New Jersey common law, condonation has been statutorily abolished (*see below*, "Defenses to Divorce," for further treatment).

Indignities

This claim includes (i) addiction to narcotics (for at least twelve consecutive months counted after the marriage); (ii) habitual drunkenness (for at least twelve consecutive months counted after the marriage), and (iii) intentional deviant sexual conduct without the victim spouse's consent (requires no waiting period).

Imprisonment

The defendant spouse must be imprisoned for at least eighteen consecutive months. Counting on the eighteen months begins after the couple marries.

Institutionalization

The defendant must be institutionalized for mental illness for a period of twenty four or more consecutive months, which begins to be counted subsequent to the marriage.

Irreconcilable Differences

Irreconcilable differences was instituted in 2007 as a new cause of action for divorce. It permits divorce in cases where irreconcilable differences have caused the breakdown of the marriage in such a way that there is no reasonable prospect of reconciliation. The statute requires marital breakdown for a period of six months prior to the concession of the divorce.

DEFENSES TO DIVORCE

If the defendant decides to contest the divorce, a trial will be held where the plaintiff will have the burden of proving one of the fault grounds of divorce. Even if the plaintiff meets her burden, the defendant may successfully oppose the divorce if he establishes one of the defenses to divorce. These defenses are rooted in the case law.[57] Although § 2A:34-7 of the New Jersey Statutes has abolished recrimination, condonation, and the clean hands doctrine, nothing in the statutes suggests that provocation, connivance, or collusion has been abolished.

The defenses to divorce are as follow:

- **Connivance** refers to the encouragement or participation of one spouse in the other spouse's wrongdoing. To successfully invoke this defense, the defending spouse must show that the plaintiff somehow set up or encouraged the defending spouse's wrongdoing. The defense of connivance can be invoked if, for example, the defending spouse shows that the plaintiff, who is suing for divorce on the basis of the defendant's habitual drunkenness, routinely purchased and left open bottles of liquor in plain view of the defendant, who was struggling with alcoholism.
- **Provocation** can be invoked when the defendant can show that the plaintiff provoked the defendant's wrongdoing. This defense is used especially in cases of divorce based on abuse and abandonment.
- **Collusion** refers to a conspiracy for fraudulent purposes between the spouses. It serves as a defense when the defendant establishes that the fault grounds for the divorce were fabricated by the parties in order to obtain an

---

[57] *See McChesney v. McChesney*, 91 N.J. Super. 523 (N.J. Super. Ct. 1966).

immediate divorce without having to wait out the statutory period required of no-fault divorce (*see infra.*).

Recrimination, condonation, and the clean hands doctrine traditionally served as defenses in New Jersey divorce actions, particularly those based on adultery. All three, however, have been abolished by statute.[58]

- **Recrimination** refers to the defendant's countercharge that the plaintiff is guilty of the same conduct for which the plaintiff is bringing the divorce action. For example, the defense can be invoked by the defendant in an action for divorce based on adultery if she can prove that the plaintiff also engaged in adultery.
- **Condonation** is invoked when the defendant proves that his spouse condoned his conduct and thus waived her right to sue based on that conduct. Condonation includes both *explicit forgiving* and *implied consent* of the behavior. Implied consent can be established by a showing that the plaintiff resumed full marital relations after the offensive behavior had been committed. Implied consent is in many ways like the defense of *reconciliation*, a defense recognized in many states that blocks a divorce when the defendant shows that the plaintiff resumed full marital relations after learning of the defendant's offense.
- **The Clean Hands Doctrine** prohibits a party from seeking relief or asserting a defense "if that party has violated an equitable principle."[59] A court will not grant a divorce to a plaintiff who has acted unfairly or immorally with respect to the marriage.

NO-FAULT DIVORCE

No-fault divorce, which is sometimes referred to as divorce by separation, requires two elements to be met:

---

[58] N.J. Rev. Stat. § 2A:34-7.
[59] *Black's Law Dictionary* 268 (8th ed. 2004).

- *No Reasonable Prospect for Reconciliation*. First, there must be **no reasonable prospect for reconciliation**. This entails more than the routine difficulties that typically accompany marriage; the breakdown must be severe. In *Anderson v. Anderson*,[60] the court held that the breakdown was not sufficiently severe when the plaintiff alleged, "we was married approximately six months before my incarceration and a few months before my incarceration things was beginning to fade, fade a little bit, you know. It wasn't exactly like it was when we first got married."
- *Separation*. Second, the spouses must have lived apart for a period of at least **eighteen consecutive months**. The complaint cannot be filed until the eighteen month waiting period has elapsed.

Because it can be economically difficult for the spouses to maintain separate residences during the no-fault divorce waiting period, many will instead opt for fault-based divorce on the grounds of irreconcilable differences, since it requires no separation and only an assertion that irreconcilable differences existed for the period of six months prior to the filing of the complaint.

Only one spouse is required to leave the marital home, live apart for the statutory period, and claim irreconcilable differences in order to obtain the divorce by separation.

Defense to divorce on the grounds of a reasonable prospect for reconciliation will usually be of no avail; the mere disagreement as to whether there are irreconcilable differences will often serve as evidence of the irreconcilable differences. No-fault divorce thus enables one spouse to unilaterally seek divorce without the fault or approval of the other spouse. This is known as "victim divorce" when the other spouse opposes the divorce, is not at fault for the separation, and can do nothing to stop it.

---

[60] *Anderson v. Anderson*, 122 N.J. Super. 285 (N.J. Super. Ct. 1973).

MEDIATION

Mediation is a process where a mediator, or neutral third party, listens to both sides of a controversy and facilitates negotiations between the parties in order to reach a voluntary agreement resolving their conflict.[61] Mediators, unlike arbitrators, do not make binding decisions for the parties. Rather, they speak to both parties and try to arrive to a mutually agreed-to compromise. They may provide the parties with additional channels of communication or propose solutions.

New Jersey's mediation rules, governed by N.J. Rev. Stat. § 2A:23C-1 to 23C-10, are based on the Uniform Mediation Act, a model statute that has been enacted in nine states.[62] In New Jersey, it was signed into law and became effective on November 22, 2004.[63]

Mediation may serve spouses by helping them to resolve differences without needing to take recourse to divorce. Spouses are not required to come to an agreement during mediation and neither party is bound to accept the suggestions of the mediator. The parties may not be forced to submit to mediation and either participant may leave mediation at any time, regardless of whether the dispute was resolved.

Despite these limitations, mediation can serve as an effective tool in helping a couple resolve differences and overcome other problems when both spouses are committed to doing so.

---

[61] N.J. Rev. Stat. § 2A:23C-2.
[62] Association for Conflict Resolution, ACR and the Uniform Mediation Act (UMA), available at <http://www.acrnet.org/uma/index.htm>.
[63] "Uniform Mediation Act," *LexBlog*, available at <http://www.njlawblog.com/client-alerts-uniform-mediation-act.html>.

5.

FINANCIAL CONSEQUENCES OF DIVORCE

THE DIVISION OF PROPERTY: EQUITABLE DISTRIBUTION

Introduction

There are two approaches to property division in divorce actions in the United States; every state has adopted either the community property (also known as *marital property*) or equitable distribution (also known as *separate property*) approach. New Jersey, like the majority of states, has adopted the separate property approach. Within this approach, all *marital property* is divided between the parties according to a set of factors encompassed in the equitable distribution scheme (*see infra.*).

The separate property approach adopted by New Jersey can be contrasted with the marital property approach, where marital property (property legally or beneficially acquired during the marriage, regardless of who holds title) is split according to equitable distribution factors. Many of the separate property exceptions in the separate property approach as to what constitutes marital property, such as personal injury awards to one spouse, are also excluded from marital property in community property states. However, community property states employ a different set of guidelines. For example, in California, a community property state, the mere use and representation of transmutation is an insufficient basis for the transformation of separate property into marital property. Unlike in separate property states, in California, a written agreement is necessary for the operation of transmutation.

The following states have adopted the community property approach: Arizona, California, Idaho, Louisiana, Nevada, New Mexico, Texas, Washington, and Wisconsin.

Distinguishing Marital Property from Separate Property

Defining Marital Property

Introduction

Marital property is defined as all property legally acquired by the parties *during the marriage*, regardless of how title is held, with some exceptions, such as gifts, inheritances, and personal injury awards awarded to only one of the spouses. Marital property can be distinguished from separate property, which is defined as any property brought into the marriage by either party prior to the marriage or which was awarded to only one of the spouses during the marriage (*e.g.*, a gift intended for only one of the spouses that was given during the marriage).

Future Property

Marital property includes all property acquired during the marriage, and *does not include future income*. Therefore, the value of future income based on a professional degree obtained during the marriage may not be used in calculating equitable distribution. New Jersey thus follows the ***majority approach*** with respect to the calculation of marital property for the purpose of equitable distribution: *future property is not marital property*.

This was made clear in the case *Mahoney v. Mahoney*,[64] where the plaintiff filed for divorce from the defendant, who had supported the marriage for sixteen months while the plaintiff pursued his MBA. The defendant sought reimbursement for the support she provided while the plaintiff pursued his degree. The court held that the plaintiff's degree was not marital property and therefore may not be distributed as such. However, since the defendant's contribution to the plaintiff's professional degree was made with

---

[64] *Mahoney v. Mahoney*, 453 A.2d 527 (N.J. 1982).

the expectation of deriving future benefits, equity entitled the defendant to reimbursement alimony.

This case can be compared with *O'Brien v. O'Brien*,[65] which demonstrates the contrasting approach taken by New York State, which follows the minority approach as to future income. The Court held that the plaintiff's medical license was marital property as long as the defendant relinquished opportunities so that the plaintiff could pursue the degree.

The Transformation of Separate Property into Marital Property

Some property may be classified by a court as marital property or may come to be transformed into marital property by the title holder even if it was acquired prior to the marriage. This may occur through either *transmutation* or *commingling*.

Transmutation. Though rarely invoked in New Jersey, this doctrine causes separate property to become transformed into marital property. Although it is not dealt with in detail in the New Jersey common law, there appears to be two elements: (i) the transformation must occur through *use* of the separate property; and (ii) the title-holding spouse must represent to the other party that the separate property is to be *shared* and *treated* as marital property.[66]

For example, a home that one spouse inherited would become marital property if the inheriting spouse tells the other that the home is to be used as their marital home and the couple moves into the home and uses it as the marital home.

Commingling. Separate property can also be transformed into marital property through commingling, which occurs when the following elements are met: (i) the title-holding spouse *mixes* his separate property with the marital property (or with the other spouse's separate property); and (ii) the title-holding spouse *intends* for the separate property to be transmuted into marital property. Thus, if separate property is sold and the proceeds are

---

[65] *O'Brien v. O'Brien*, 498 N.Y.S. 743 (1985).
[66] *Coney v. Coney*, 207 N.J. Super. 63, 75, 503 A.2d 912 (Ch. Div. 1985).

mixed with the marital property by placing them in a joint bank account, the funds will remain separate property if the parties did not intend for the proceeds to become marital property.

An example of commingling would be if one party gives to the other the proceeds from a personal injury award with the intent that it be used to purchase a residence in their joint names, and it is used for that purpose.

The presumption that separate property has been transmuted into marital property is rebuttable.[67]

Defining Separate Property

Some property is not classified as marital property even if it has been acquired during the marriage. Such property, called "separate property," is not equitably distributed upon divorce. Such property includes the following:

-    *Gifts*. Property that is given as a gift to one spouse is excluded from equitable distribution. However, this does not include inter-spousal gifts made during the marriage, which are equitably distributed;
-    *Intestate successions of either party*. Property that either spouse inherited through an intestate succession is not equitably distributed[68];
-    *Personal injury claims*. This rule comes not from statutes, but from the case law, which excludes personal injury claims from equitable distribution.[69] This policy is based on the view that one spouse's pain and suffering is not shared by the other spouse. It was not always the case in New Jersey. In *DiTolvo v. DiTolvo*,[70] the court allowed a personal injury claim to be divided as marital property, but the policy was changed in later cases, principally *Petersen v.*

---

[67] *In re Marriage of Smith*, 86 Ill. 2d 518, 530, 427 N.E.2d 1239 (Ill. 1981).

[68] N.J. Rev. Stat. § 2A:34-23.

[69] *See Landwehr v. Landwehr*, 111 N.J. 491 (1988).

[70] *DiTolvo v. DiTolvo*, 131 N.J. Super. 72 (App. Div. 1974).

Petersen.[71] Today, personal injury awards are excluded from equitable distribution; and

- *Tracing*. Property whose origins can be traced to separate property is excluded from equitable distribution. If, for example, one party acquires property during the marriage but can show that the property was acquired through the sale of separate property, a court may classify the property as separate property not subject to equitable distribution.

The Application of Equitable Distribution

In a divorce proceeding, marital property is divided between the parties on an equitable basis. Thus, unlike in community property states, property in New Jersey is not automatically split equally. Rather, **equitable distribution** is used to apply a series of factors in order to determine how marital property should be split equitably. In practice, there is an equal division of assets in most cases, but wide variation is possible given the specific factors of particular cases. It is also important to note that equitable distribution divides not only the marital property acquired during the marriage, but the marital debts acquired during the marriage as well.

Factors

Several factors are used in determining the equitable distribution of property. Many of these are the same as those used in determining alimony, including:

- The standard of living during the marriage;
- The economic needs of each spouse;
- The duration of the marriage;
- The contribution of each spouse to the marriage, including both financial and non-financial contributions, such as contributions to the education of the other spouse;
- The age, physical, and emotional health of the parties;
- The wage-earning capacities and employability of the parties;
- The parental responsibilities for the children;

---

[71] *Petersen v. Petersen*, 85 N.J. 638 (1981).

- Interruption of educational or career opportunities; and
- Any other factors relevant in the court's judgment.[72]

Other factors used exclusively in determining equitable distribution include the following:

- The property that each party brought into the marriage; and
- Any agreement that the parties had on property distribution from before they entered into the marriage.[73]

The Effect of Adultery

Equitable distribution, like alimony, is not automatically barred when one of the spouses engaged in adultery or some other wrongful act. Furthermore, adultery or any other wrongdoing is not listed anywhere in the equitable distribution statute as a factor that may be used in determining the equitable distribution of property. However, it is possible that acts involving extreme and egregious misbehavior fall into the court's consideration as "[a]ny other factors that the court may deem relevant."[74] Such misbehavior may include adultery.

Yet when considering misbehavior or adultery as a factor for equitable distribution, a court is likely to take into account only misbehavior so unusually egregious that it offends the social contract. Courts have a similar approach when considering adultery and misbehavior in determining alimony.[75]

ALIMONY (SPOUSAL SUPPORT)

Introduction

In New Jersey, alimony refers to the permanent or temporary payments that one spouse provides to the other pending judgment or after judgment of any matrimonial action (divorce or divorce

---

[72] N.J. Rev. Stat. § 2A:34-23.1 (2006).
[73] Id.
[74] Id. § 2A:34-23.
[75] Mani v. Mani, 183 N.J. 70 (2005).

from bed and board). Alimony is an allowance for living expenses that one spouse is ordered to pay the other.

Historically, alimony referred only to the husband's duty to support the wife. However, the U.S. Supreme Court has held that statutes requiring only husbands to pay spousal support (alimony) violate the Equal Protection Clause and are unconstitutional. Today, spousal support must be awarded to the economically dependent spouse, regardless of his gender.

This rule was established in *Orr v. Orr*,[76] where Lillian Orr sued her ex-husband William Orr for failure to pay her alimony after they were divorced. The defendant argued that the Alabama statute that required only husbands to pay alimony was unconstitutional in that it denied equal protection under the laws by discriminating on the basis of gender. The U.S. Supreme Court agreed and ruled in his favor.

As a result of *Orr v. Orr*, many states today use the term "spousal support" rather than "alimony" to refer to one spouse's support of the dependent spouse. The New Jersey statutes, however, continue to use the more traditional term "alimony." However, when referencing "alimony," the statutes are actually referring to gender-neutral spousal support and are not meant to indicate that only the husband can be required to pay. The present text uses "alimony" and "spousal support" interchangeably.

Distinguished from Equitable Distribution

Alimony is distinct from the equitable distribution of marital property. While equitable distribution occurs only once when the parties dissolve the marital bonds, alimony continues for as long as there is need.

The national trend is to replace alimony with the division of property upon dissolution of marriage and to leave out alimony entirely. In New Jersey, alimony applies in addition to equitable distribution.

---

[76] *Orr v. Orr*, 440 U.S. 268 (1979).

Factors for the Determination of Alimony

Alimony seeks to balance the preservation of the pre-divorce standard of living of each party against the paying spouse's financial means. Thus, the pre-divorce standard of living and the means of the paying spouse are two key factors used in determining spousal support.

In making its ruling on alimony, the court will consider the circumstances of the parties and the nature of the case while assuring that alimony will cover the medical and possible educational expenses of the dependent spouse.[77]

The courts will take into account a host of factors when determining the amount of alimony to be paid. Many of these factors are the same as those used in determining equitable distribution of marital property. Among those factors are as follow:

- The standard of living achieved during the marriage;
- The economic needs of each spouse;
- The duration of the marriage;
- The contribution of each spouse to the marriage, including both financial and non-financial contributions, such as contributions to the education of the other spouse;
- The age, physical, and emotional health of the parties;
- The wage-earning capacity and employability of each of the spouses;
- The parental responsibilities for the children;
- Interruption of educational or career opportunities; and
- Any other factors relevant in the court's judgment.[78]

Among the factors that the courts consider that are used for determining alimony but *not* for equitable distribution, we can highlight:

- The time and expenses necessary for the dependent spouse to become employable; and
- Any equitable distribution awarded.[79]

---

[77] N.J. Rev. Stat. § 2A:34-23.
[78] *Id.* § 2A:34-23.

A loss of income by the paying spouse will reduce the amount of alimony that he is ordered to pay. However, *voluntary* behavior that contributes to a loss of income will lessen the impact of this reduction. For example, if a spouse voluntarily refuses to seek employment, *a minimum salary may be imputed* on him for the purposes of a determination of the alimony he will be required to pay.

As with equitable distribution, adultery and other misbehavior will normally not be used as a factor in determining alimony. However, when the misbehavior or adultery either causes the dependent spouse to gain financially or the paying spouse to experience financial detriment, or when the misbehavior is so egregious that it violates the social contract, the conduct may be used as a factor in determining alimony.[80]

Thus, unlike in some states, where adultery bars the dependent spouse from receiving alimony, in New Jersey, adultery does not act as an automatic bar. Rather, it can only be used as a *factor* in determining alimony, and even then, it will only be used in limited circumstances.

Termination of Alimony

Alimony is terminated when any of the following circumstances arise:

- *Remarriage of the dependent spouse.* This applies to cases of both permanent and temporary alimony. However, the remarriage of the dependent spouse does not necessarily terminate rehabilitative or reimbursement alimony, unless the court finds that "the circumstances upon which the [alimony] award was based have not occurred or unless the payer spouse demonstrates an agreement or good cause to the contrary."[81]

---

[79] *Id.*
[80] *Mani v. Mani* (N.J. 2005).
[81] N.J. Rev. Stat. § 2A:34-25.

-   *Death of either spouse.*[82] To protect the dependent spouse from the termination of alimony through death of the paying spouse, the paying spouse may be required to establish a trust fund or to make the dependent spouse the beneficiary of the paying spouse's life insurance.[83]

Nothing in the statutes suggests that the dependent spouse's entry into sexual relations or cohabitation with a new partner necessarily bars the continued receipt of alimony. However, as we will see below, if such cohabitation or relations impact the economic necessity of the dependent spouse, the court may reduce the amount of alimony to be paid.

Modification of Alimony

Alimony may be modified as a result of changes in the economic circumstances of either the dependent or the paying spouse, including any of the following: (i) an increase or decrease in the salary of the paying spouse; (ii) changes in costs of living; (iii) employment by the dependent spouse that permits self-support; and (iv) increases in the costs of the children.[84] Furthermore, cohabitation of the dependent spouse with another person may result in a decrease in alimony payments if the cohabitation leads to reduced costs of living for the dependant spouse.[85]

Not all changed circumstances lead to modifications of alimony. If, for example, the paying spouse voluntarily leaves his job or retires early, he will not necessarily be permitted to abate alimony payments.[86]

In this way, alimony is like child support and child custody, which may also be modified based on changed circumstances, and is unlike equitable distribution, which is not subject to modification once it is ordered.

---

[82] *See Jacobson v. Jacobson*, 146 N.J. Super. 491 (Ch. Div. 1976).
[83] *Davis v. Davis*, 184 N.J. Super. 430 (App. Div. 1982).
[84] *Lepis v. Lepis*, 83 N.J. 139 (1980).
[85] *Gayet v. Gayet*, 92 N.J. 149 (1983).
[86] *Dilger v. Dilger*, 242 N.J. Super. 380 (Ch. Div. 1990).

Classes of Alimony

Pendente Lite (Temporary) Alimony

Because the party filing for divorce may lack the resources to maintain a separate household during the period between when he files for divorce[87] and the period when the divorce is granted, the courts have the power to order the defendant to pay *pendente lite* alimony to the plaintiff. *Pendente lite* alimony is a form of alimony that is to be paid to the dependent spouse during the litigation in order to assure that his basic needs are met. The court is to use equity in rewarding alimony or maintenance in a way that is just and fit.[88]

Rehabilitative Alimony

The New Jersey common law recognizes rehabilitative spousal support, a form of support generally available when the couple was married for only a short period and the dependent spouse would be capable of gaining employment based on training or education. Under this form of spousal support, the paying spouse is required to pay the dependent spouse only during the time that the dependent spouse would require to become fully self-sufficient and self-dependent.[89] The payee must show the scope of rehabilitation, the steps to be taken, and the employment to be taken while the rehabilitation occurs.[90]

The quantity of rehabilitative spousal support to be paid is determined through the same factors used in determining alimony, *pendente lite* alimony, and separate maintenance.[91]

SEPARATE MAINTENANCE

Separate maintenance is "[m]oney paid by one married person to another for support if they are no longer living together as husband

---

[87] Including divorce from bed and board and annulment.

[88] N.J. Rev. Stat. § 2A:34-23.

[89] *Heinl v. Heinl*, 287 N.J. Super. 337 (App. Div. 1996).

[90] N.J. Rev. Stat. § 2A.23-23.

[91] *Id.* § 2A:34-23.

and wife."[92] In some States, a person may be required to pay separate maintenance to his spouse even if he continues to live with her. Virginia is one such state. In New Jersey, separate maintenance is like alimony in that the spouses must be separated by living apart or by judicial decree, as in the case of divorce from bed and board, in order for separate maintenance to be ordered.

Separate maintenance can be used as a means for a dependent spouse to support himself as well as his children,[93] and the only requirements for obtaining separate maintenance are: (i) the parties live in separate dwellings; and (ii) one of the spouses demonstrate financial need. The factors used in determining separate maintenance payments are the same as those used in determining alimony.[94]

The main difference between separate maintenance and alimony is that separate maintenance can be awarded without the recipient spouse's having been divorced or without his seeking to obtain a divorce. Alimony, by contrast, with the exception of *pendente lite* alimony, actually requires a divorce order before it is paid.[95]

TAX CONSEQUENCES OF ALIMONY, SEPARATE MAINTENANCE, AND CHILD SUPPORT

When a spouse is ordered to pay alimony or separate maintenance under a divorce or separate maintenance decree, she may receive a tax deduction equal to the amount paid from her gross income.[96] The receiving spouse would then claim the payments as taxable income.

In contrast, no tax deduction is permitted for payments of child support. The payments are taxed directly from the paying spouse's

---

[92] *Black's Law Dictionary*, "separate maintenance" (8th ed. 2004).
[93] DivorceNet – New Jersey Separation Agreements, available at <http://www.divorcenet.com/states/new_jersey/new_jersey_separation_a greements>.
[94] *See* N.J. Rev. Stat. § 2A:34-23.
[95] *Isserman v. Isserman*, 11 N.J. 106 (1952).
[96] *Id.* § 54A: 3-2.

income and the beneficiary child receives the payments free of taxation.

REAL PROPERTY

Spouses hold real property jointly as a tenancy by the entirety. Recognized in only twenty states, a tenancy by the entirety can be likened to a joint tenancy, except that it includes the extra element of marriage. Under this form of tenancy, if either spouse wishes to alienate the property, he may do so only with the consent of the other.

If either spouse dies, title of the property automatically vests with the surviving spouse. When the couple divorces, the tenancy by the entirety is severed and becomes a tenancy in common, where each co-tenant's share of the property is separate and distinct and each co-tenant may dispose of his undivided share, by deed or by will.

6.

DOMESTIC VIOLENCE

THE PREVENTION OF DOMESTIC VIOLENCE ACT

Recognizing that domestic violence is a serious issue in New Jersey, that the elderly as well as children are affected by it, and that thousands of New Jersey citizens were beaten, tortured, or killed by their spouses, the New Jersey Legislature passed the Prevention of Domestic Violence Act of 1991 (PDVA).[97]

The PDVA protects against domestic violence, defined in New Jersey as the occurrence of homicide, assault, terrorist threats, kidnapping, criminal restraint, false imprisonment, criminal sexual contact, lewdness, criminal mischief, burglary, criminal trespass, harassment, or stalking by an emancipated minor or adult. To qualify as an act of domestic violence under the PDVA, the victim must be either:

- an *adult* or *emancipated minor* who: (i) is or was the abuser's spouse; or (ii) is or was living in the same household as the abuser; or
- *any person, regardless of age*, who: (i) has a child in common with the abuser or who is expecting to have a child in common with the abuser; or (ii) has or has had a dating relationship with the abuser.[98]

By passing the PDVA, the Legislature intended to "assure the victims of domestic violence the maximum protection from abuse

---

[97] N.J. Rev. Stat. § 2C:25-17 *et. seq.*
[98] *Id.* § 2C:25-19.

the law can provide."[99] The PDVA provides victims of domestic violence with both civil relief in the form of a restraining order and criminal relief by allowing the filing of criminal complaints against the abuser. Moreover, certain offenders must pay a civil penalty of $50 to $500,[100] which is to be forwarded to the Domestic Violence Victims' Fund.[101]

In imposing this civil penalty, the court shall take into consideration the nature and degree of injury suffered by the victim. The court may waive the penalty in cases of extreme financial hardship

LAW ENFORCEMENT PROCEDURES

When a law enforcement officer responds to a domestic violence call, his primary duty is to enforce the law and protect the victim. He must give the victim a notice in English and in Spanish explaining the victim's rights under the PDVA, including the rights to a temporary or final restraining order. The law enforcement officer must also complete a domestic violence offense report, which is forwarded to the Municipal Court where the offense was committed or to the Superior Court.[102]

When a law enforcement officer, responding to an incident, has reason to believe that domestic violence has occurred, he may arrest the abuser and sign a complaint against him. If the victim shows evidence of injury or if there is probable cause that the attacker either violated a restraining order or used a weapon in attacking the victim, the officer must arrest the attacker.

RIGHTS UNDER THE ACT

Victims of domestic abuse may file a criminal complaint or a civil complaint against the abuser. Criminal complaints could lead to the imprisonment or other punishment of the abuser. Civil complaints,

---

[99] *Id.* § 2C:25-18.
[100] *Id.* § 2C:25-29.1.
[101] *Id.* § 2C:25-29.2.
[102] *Id.* § 2C:25-24.

which are filed in the Family Part of the Chancery Division of the New Jersey Superior Court or in a Municipal Court, may lead to civil remedies, such as civil restraining orders against the abuser. In addition, victims of domestic violence may file for protective orders, temporary restraining orders, and final restraining orders.

Reasonable force in self-defense is not to be construed as prosecutable violence under the PDVA. No one who in self-defense resisted an attacker can be charged under the Act.[103]

RESTRAINING ORDERS UNDER THE ACT

Introduction

A victim of domestic violence may seek a restraining order in order to enjoin the defendant from harassing, threatening, or contacting her in any way. The order may be used to keep the attacker away from the scene of abuse, whether it is the workplace or home of the victim or some other place.

A party seeking a restraining order may do so in the Family Part of the Chancery Division. To obtain a restraining order for domestic violence, the applicant must prove the applicant was the victim of domestic violence by a co-habitant, a parent of a child in common, or a current or former dating partner. Otherwise, the victim may be able to obtain a restraining order under some other law, such as the criminal law on stalking.

Temporary Restraining Orders

Overview

Temporary restraining orders may be granted to protect the life and well-being of victims of abuse. When emergency relief is necessary, the judge may award an *ex parte* temporary restraining order, which does not notify the party being bound or grant him the opportunity to be heard.[104] Such restraining orders may be granted when

---

[103] *Id.* § 2C:25-21.
[104] *Id.* § 2C:25-28f-g.

necessary for protecting victims from further abuse or ensuring prompt action in times of danger.

The temporary restraining order may protect the victim in the following ways:

- By prohibiting the defendant from entering the victim's home;
- By prohibiting the defendant from having contact with the victim or her family, including a prohibition from contacting the victim's children until a risk-evaluation is done;
- By requiring the defendant to reimburse the victim for any costs resulting from the abuse, such as the cost of moving away;
- By granting temporary custody of the children to the victim; and
- By requiring the defendant to pay the victim for medical expenses associated with abuse and for temporary child support.[105]

Procedure

The victim must file a complaint petitioning the court for a temporary restraining order. Within ten days, a hearing is held. The general rule is that the victim must appear before the judge and give testimony. However, in some cases, the testimony may be presented to the judge via electronic communication. If the temporary restraining order is granted, the defendant may immediately appeal through a *de novo* hearing. If the temporary restraining order is sustained, a follow-up hearing will be held to determine whether the order should be extended into a final (permanent) restraining order.

Enforcement

A copy of the temporary restraining order is to be delivered on the defendant by the police or sheriff.[106] If the defendant violates the

---

[105] *Id.* § 2C:25-23.

order, the victim should inform the police, who can arrest the defendant and charge him with criminal contempt of court, which carries a jail sentence.

Final Restraining Orders

A court may enter a final restraining order against a person who committed an act of domestic violence if there is sufficient proof of abuse based on the preponderance of the evidence standard. The court will consider the following factors:

-   The history of violence between the parties;
-   The existence of immediate danger and the protection of the victim;
-   The financial circumstances of the plaintiff and defendant;
-   The best interests of the victim and potentially the child;
-   In determining custody and parenting time, the protection of the victim's safety; and
-   Whether another jurisdiction has entered a restraining order.[107]

A restraining order may be modified or dissolved if the parties are reconciled or for good cause shown, with the court's consideration of the need for possible continued protection. The parties must apply to the Family Part of the Chancery Division, and be heard by the same judge who originally entered the restraining order or by another judge with a complete record.[108]

THE FEDERAL VIOLENCE AGAINST WOMEN ACT

The federal Violence Against Women Act of 2000 (VAWA) also provides protections to female victims of violence through enhanced investigation and prosecution of violent crimes against women and allowing for civil redress when cases are not criminally prosecuted.

---

[106] *Id.* § 2C:25-28(12)l.
[107] *Id.* § 2C:25-29.
[108] *Id.* § 2C:25-29d.

Under VAWA, a person who is awarded a restraining order in one state and later comes to New Jersey is guaranteed full faith and credit; the restraining order will be honored in New Jersey. A victim holding a restraining order may take any of the following steps:

- Automatically have New Jersey recognize the restraining order without taking action;
- Have the restraining order declared valid by a New Jersey court; or
- Seek a separate restraining order from New Jersey.

EVIDENCE AND MARITAL PRIVILEGES

The marital communications privilege applies to any confidential communications made between the spouses during the marriage. The privilege prohibits either spouse from testifying as to these communications in a criminal or civil case without the consent of the other. The privilege does not apply to communications made before the marriage or after a divorce (including divorce from bed and board), but communications made during the marriage continue to receive protection even after a divorce takes place. Protected communications must be *confidential*, that is, made when the spouses were alone with no third party present, with limited exceptions (*e.g.*, the third party was an infant lacking capacity).[109]

The marital communications privilege does not apply when testifying as to the existence of the marriage or to offenses committed against the spouse or child. Similarly, it does not apply to a spouse's testimony as an alibi at a criminal trial when he is subpoenaed by the other spouse.

---

[109] *Id.* § 2A:84A-22.

CHILD ABUSE, NEGLECT, AND PROTECTIVE SERVICES

New Jersey Task Force on Child Abuse and Neglect Act

The New Jersey Legislature in 1996 adopted the "New Jersey Task Force on Child Abuse and Neglect Act" (NJTF) in order to study and make recommendations regarding the best ways to improve child protective services and to create a Task Force that may apply for and distribute funds received from any governmental and non governmental agencies.[110] The Task Force will then "receive, evaluate and approve applications of public and private agencies and organizations for grants from moneys annually appropriated from the 'Children's Trust Fund.'"[111]

Task Force members chair several subcommittees that include representatives of New Jersey state departments and public and private organizations. These subcommittees include the Protection Subcommittee, the Prevention Subcommittee, the Communication Subcommittee, and the Staffing and Oversight Subcommittee.[112]

Comprehensive Child Abuse Prevention and Treatment Act.

The New Jersey Legislature further adopted the "Comprehensive Child Abuse Prevention and Treatment Act"[113] (CAPTA). Under this Act, a Commissioner of Children and Families, appointed by the Governor, establishes rules and procedures for responding to instances of medical neglect, such as the withholding of medically necessary treatment from disabled children.[114]

The Act establishes a Child Fatality and Near Fatality Review Board, within the Department of Children and Families, in order to review and analyze the causes of fatalities and near fatalities as well as their potential means of prevention.[115]

---

[110] *See* N.J. Rev. Stat. § 9:6-8.74, *et. seq.*
[111] N.J. Rev. Stat. §§ 9:6-8.74, 81.
[112] State of New Jersey Department of Children and Families, available at <http://www.state.nj.us/dcf/about/commissions/njtfcan>.
[113] *See* N.J. Rev. Stat. § 9:6-8.83, *et. seq.*
[114] N.J. Rev. Stat. § 9:6-8.85.
[115] *Id.* § 9:6-8.88.

The New Jersey Commissioner of Children and Families has established four regional diagnostic treatment centers for child abuse and neglect, as required by the Act.[116] The centers provide identification and diagnosis of child abuse, psychological and social services, medical consultations, expert testimony in court hearings, and the services of lawyers. The centers employ doctors, psychologists, social workers, and lawyers who work cooperatively in enforcing the law in a way that minimizes trauma for the children.[117]

Parens Patriae

Normally, the state does not have standing to sue on behalf of citizens. There are, however, some exceptions, one of which applies when a citizen lacks the ability to prosecute the lawsuit because of infancy, mental incompetence, or some other cause. In such a situation, the doctrine of *parens patriae* arises, granting the state standing to prosecute.[118] For example, the New Jersey courts are granted *parens patriae* jurisdiction over a child when she is kidnapped by one parent and taken out of the state.

The state is given jurisdiction over custody and maintenance of children who are residents of New Jersey, regardless of domicile. This is based on the common law concept that the state owes protection to the incompetent and the helpless.[119] The Attorney General may initiate a suit to commit any person to the custody of the state under the state's *parens patriae* jurisdiction.[120]

---

[116] *Id.* § 9:6-8.99.
[117] American Academy of Pediatricians, available at <http://www.aap.org/sections/scan/medicaldiagnostic/newjersey.htm>.
[118] *Black's Law Dictionary* 1144 "parens patriae" (8th ed. 2004).
[119] *Fantony v. Fantony*, 21 N.J. 525, 531, 122 A.2d 593, 598 (1956).
[120] N.J. Rev. Stat. § 30:4-27.28.

7.

ABORTION

UNITED STATES CONSTITUTIONAL BACKGROUND

Abortion is perhaps the most controversial subject in American family law. From arguments on the morality of having an abortion, to discussions on whether the U.S. Constitution recognizes a woman's right to choose abortion, to questions on the personhood of the fetus, abortion has been the subject of much heated debate over recent decades. Justice Blackmun, who wrote the landmark decision of *Roe v. Wade*,[121] considered the opinion to be his *magnum opus*, one that would finally and forever put an end to the abortion debate. Far from achieving that vision, the infamous case came to the fore of a major division in American political life and fanned the flames of the abortion controversy.

The decision had a great impact on the lives of American women. After *Roe*, every state was required to recognize the right of a woman to choose an abortion during the first trimester. During the second and third trimesters, state regulations had to be reasonable. Laws that banned a woman's right to choose an abortion were held to be unconstitutional, even if they allowed for exceptions to protect the life or health of the mother. Such bans were held to violate women's constitutional liberty rights.

The Trimester Approach of *Roe v. Wade*

In *Roe v. Wade*, the plaintiff, a pregnant unmarried woman, sought an abortion in Texas, where abortion was illegal except when

---

[121] Roe v. Wade, 410 U.S. 113 (1973).

necessary to save the mother's life. The plaintiff Roe sued the county district attorney Wade for a declaratory judgment stating that the law was discriminatory on its face. She also sought an injunction against the enforcement of the law. The Court ruled in her favor, holding that the Texas law unconstitutionally violated the right to privacy and granting the injunction. The Court reasoned that although the Constitution does not explicitly create a right to privacy, the right is implied in the First, Fourth, Fifth, and Ninth Amendments, as well as in the Liberty Clause of the Fourteenth Amendment.

The Court affirmed that statutes infringing on the privacy right are subject to the most rigorous standard of constitutional scrutiny: they must be necessary to protect a compelling state interest. Many arguments have been put forward defending the state interests supported by anti-abortion laws, and the Court dealt with each one of them in turn: some argue that such laws protect the woman from invasive, unsafe procedures, but these procedures are much safer today; others argue that such laws protect against illicit sexual relations, but the relationship between such relations and abortion restrictions are quite attenuated; finally, some argue that anti-abortion laws protect fetal life, but the Fourteenth Amendment protects only post-natal life. Thus, no compelling state interest was found in support of abortion bans.

The Court then guaranteed the right of women to choose to have an abortion during the first trimester. States may, however, reasonably regulate abortion procedures during the second trimester in order to protect the woman undergoing the abortion. However, states may not regulate the *decision* to have an abortion in the second trimester. In the third trimester, when the fetus becomes viable outside of the womb, states, in promoting their interest in protecting "the potentiality of human life," may regulate procedures and may even prohibit abortions. However, such bans must allow for exceptions to protect the life or health of the mother.

The *Roe* holding has had a profound impact. After the Court handed down its decision, anti-abortion laws throughout the nation were invalidated. However, just a few months after *Roe* was decided, the Supreme Court would again decide another abortion case whose holding would greatly expand the woman's right to an abortion. *Doe v. Bolton*[122] held that the "life or health" exception for third trimester abortion bans must include not only exceptions for the woman's physical health, but also, her emotional and psychological health. The effect was to greatly expand the right to abortion, since the woman's psychological health was to be determined by the woman and her abortionist, not according to an objective standard. The physician, in determining whether an abortion was necessary for the patient's health, could employ factors including not only the woman's general health and age, but also her emotional and familial circumstances.

The Undue Burden Test of *Planned Parenthood v. Casey*

In 1992, *Planned Parenthood of Southeastern Pennsylvania v. Casey*[123] reached the United States Supreme Court. Without overruling *Roe*, the Court abandoned many of its holdings, including the premise that that abortion is a fundamental right falling under strict scrutiny, and replaced *Roe's* trimester approach with an "undue burden" test.

In *Casey*, Planned Parenthood sued Pennsylvania Governor Casey for an injunction and declaratory relief from the Pennsylvania Abortion Control Act of 1982, which required women to give informed consent prior to an abortion and made it necessary for them to receive certain specified information twenty four hours in advance. In addition, the Act required parental consent for minors seeking an abortion and obliged married women, with some exceptions, to notify their husbands prior to getting an abortion. The Supreme Court granted *certiorari* to determine whether the Act was unconstitutional.

Justice O'Connor, in a plurality opinion, wrote that "[l]iberty finds no refuge in a jurisprudence of doubt."[124] Embracing a realist

---

[122] *Doe v. Bolton*, 410 U.S. 179 (1973).
[123] *Planned Parenthood of Southeastern Pennsylvania v. Casey*, 505 U.S. 833 (1992).
[124] *Planned Parenthood of Southeastern Pennsylvania*, 505 U.S. at 844.

worldview, she argued that where reasonable people disagree on important social policies, the government should not impose its views, for "[a]t the heart of liberty is the right to define one's own concept of existence, of meaning, of the universe, and of the mystery of human life."[125] Beliefs about these matters could not be defined "under compulsion of the State."[126] O'Connor wrote that the Fourteenth Amendment protects fundamental liberties "central to personal dignity and autonomy,"[127] and among these liberties is a woman's right to decide whether to procreate. The Constitution limits the ability of states to pass statutes that interfere with this liberty, but a state may impose reasonable regulations on this right. However, when such regulations impose an undue burden on the decision to choose, they unconstitutionally infringe on the woman's Fourteenth Amendment liberty interest.[128]

The Court held that the Pennsylvania statute generally passed the constitutional undue burden test. Today, permissible restrictions on abortion thus include the imposition of informed consent (with a twenty four hour waiting period) and parental consent requirements. The husband notification requirement, however, was held to impose an undue burden, and the case was accordingly remanded for further proceedings.

Today, anti-abortion statutes must not unduly burden the right of the mother to choose an abortion. All abortion bans must include exceptions for the life and health of the mother. These include bans on partial-birth abortions, defined as any abortion where a physician partially induces a vaginal delivery of the fetus prior to destroying and delivering the fetus.[129] In *Stenberg v. Carhart*,[130] for example, the Court struck down a Nebraska statute enacting a partial-birth abortion ban because it provided no exceptions for the health of the mother.

---

[125] *Planned Parenthood of Southeastern Pennsylvania*, 505 U.S. at 851.
[126] *Id.*
[127] *Planned Parenthood of Southeastern Pennsylvania*, 505 U.S. at 923.
[128] *Planned Parenthood of Southeastern Pennsylvania*, 505 U.S. at 874.
[129] *See Black's Law Dictionary*, "partial-birth abortion" under "abortion" (8th ed. 2004).
[130] *Stenberg v. Carhart*, 530 U.S. 914 (2000).

Severability

A statute is said to be "severable" when a court may find one provision or section to be unconstitutional, against public policy, or invalid for any other reason without striking down the entire statute. If, however, a court finds a statute to be inseverable, as is often the case when legislators state within the text of the law that a finding of invalidity as to any section of the law renders the entire section void, the court will be obligated to strike down the entire law.

The Supreme Court held recently in *Ayotte v. Planned Parenthood of Northern New England*[131] that when it is possible to separate invalid sections of an abortion law, courts should strive to sever and strike down only the invalid provisions, while preserving the rest of the law. Courts should not invalidate an entire statute when a single portion is invalid, as such a remedy would be overbroad. Rather, the courts must defer to legislatures by granting an injunction against the unconstitutional provisions of the anti-abortion statute while maintaining the rest of it intact.

NEW JERSEY'S RULES ON ABORTION REGULATION

New Jersey does not require any person, hospital, or clinic to perform abortions.[132] In fact, the New Jersey Legislature has tried on several occasions to regulate and limit abortions in the state. However, the Legislature has found its attempts to be impeded by numerous state and federal court decisions ruling them to be invalid as against the Constitution.

Partial-Birth Abortions

The New Jersey Legislature has defined partial-birth abortion as any abortion in which the delivery of the fetus is induced and the fetus is intentionally killed after being partially delivered vaginally.[133] The Legislature has tried to limit and control the

---

[131] *Ayotte v. Planned Parenthood of Northern New England*, 126 S.Ct. 961 (2006).
[132] N.J. Rev. Stat. § 2A:65A-1 to 65A-2.
[133] *Id.* § 2A:65A-6, 2.e.

number of partial birth abortions taking place within the state by passing the Partial-Birth Abortion Ban Act of 1997, which prohibited any health care professional from performing a partial-birth abortion in the state.[134] The only exceptions permitted by the ban were partial-birth abortions necessary to save the life of the mother when endangered by "a physical disorder, illness or injury."[135] The Act penalized health care professionals with the potential revocation of their professional licenses and with fines of up to $25,000.[136]

On the day the Act was to take effect, Planned Parenthood of Central New Jersey sued for a declaratory judgment against the Act and for an injunction against its enforcement. In *Planned Parenthood of Central New Jersey v. Verniero*,[137] the Act was held to be unconstitutional for vagueness and for placing an undue burden on the mother's right to choose an abortion without allowing for exceptions for the health of the mother. The court ordered a permanent injunction.

The U.S. Court of Appeals for the Third Circuit came to a similar conclusion in *Planned Parenthood of Central New Jersey v. Farmer*.[138] Citing *Roe v. Wade* and *Planned Parenthood v. Casey*, the Court held that the Act "unduly burdened a woman's constitutional right to obtain an abortion" because the language was overbroad and the Act's exception for the life of the mother, which contained no exceptions for the general health of the mother, was inadequate. The Court affirmed the permanent injunction of the District Court.

Today, the Partial-Birth Abortion Ban Act of 1997 has no validity in the state.

---

[134] *Id.* § 2A:65A-5 to -6.

[135] *Id.* § 2A:65A-6, 2.b.

[136] *Id.* § 2A:65A-6.

[137] *Planned Parenthood of Central New Jersey v. Verniero*, 41 F. Supp. 2d 478 (D.N.J. 1998).

[138] Planned Parenthood of Central New Jersey v. Farmer, 220 F.3d 127 (3d Cir. 2000).

The Parental Notification for Abortion Act

Just a few years later, the New Jersey Legislature passed the Parental Notification for Abortion Act, finding a compelling interest in protecting the family as a viable unit and the rights of parents to raise their children.[139] The Act, which was to take effect in 1999, required physicians to personally deliver notice to parents before performing abortions on unemancipated minors. Parental notification had to be given at least forty eight hours before the abortion.[140] The Act allowed for exceptions when the abortion was required in a medical emergency or when the notification was waived by petition to a Superior Court judge.[141]

Planned Parenthood of Central New Jersey sought a declaratory judgment and injunction against enforcement of the Parental Notification for Abortion Act. In *Planned Parenthood of Central New Jersey v. Farmer*,[142] the New Jersey Supreme Court concluded that the statute violated New Jersey's equal protection guarantees (implied in article I, paragraph 1 of the New Jersey Constitution) by requiring parental notification for unemancipated minors seeking abortions but not for unemancipated minors seeking other medical treatments relating to their pregnancies. Because the Legislature failed to state a substantial justification for this classification, the Court held that the Act violated equal protection.

---

[139] N.J. Rev. Stat. § 9:17A-1.2.

[140] *Id.* § 9:17A-1.4.

[141] *Id.* § 9:17A-1.6 to -1.7.

[142] *Planned Parenthood of Central New Jersey v. Farmer*, 165 N.J. 609 (2000).

8.

PARENTAGE

UNIFORM PARENTAGE ACT

The Uniform Parentage Act is a uniform law drafted by the National Conference of Commissioners of Uniform State Laws and promulgated in 2000 with amendments in 2002. The Act legally defines a child's mother and father, creates a registry for unknown and putative fathers, and allows courts to initiate genetic testing without initiating paternity suits.

Every state has adopted the Uniform Parentage Act. In New Jersey, the Act has been codified as the "New Jersey Parentage Act."[143] The Act provides procedures for determining parentage in disputed cases and for assigning child support. Abolishing distinctions between legitimate and illegitimate children, the Act "directs courts to determine rights and responsibilities based on the existence of a parent-child relationship."[144] It also determines how parentage arises in cases of assisted reproduction techniques.

Prior to the enactment of the New Jersey Parentage Act, children born to unwed mothers were disadvantaged, since the mother was considered to be the only parent. The Act changed this. Both parents of illegitimate children are now legally recognized, and children are entitled to all of the benefits owed to them by both parents, including inheritance rights and support.[145]

---

[143] N.J. Rev. Stat. § 9:17-38.
[144] *Black's Law Dictionary* 1567 (8th ed. 2004).
[145] Stephen J. Hyland, "Parenting in New Jersey: The Uncertain Legal Status of Same-Sex Couples," *Partners Task Force* (Partners Task Force for Gay & Lesbian Couples, 2006).

PRESUMED FATHERHOOD

One of the more complicated issues involved in parentage disputes is the determination paternity. While it is clear who a child's mother is, the identity of a child's father may be in doubt. Many states have passed statutes that presume a mother's husband to be her child's father when the father is neither impotent nor sterile. Although these statutes have been challenged as violating the Due Process Clause of the United States Constitution, they have been upheld by U.S. Supreme Court in various cases.

One such case is *Michael H. v. Gerald D.*,[146] where Michael H., the putative father of a young girl named Victoria, sued the mother's husband for visitation rights with Victoria. Genetic tests showed a 98% chance that the Michael H., who had an adulterous affair with the mother, was Victoria's biological father.[147] At the time, Victoria was living with her mother and her mother's husband, who were recently reconciled. Under California law, when a child is born to a married couple living together, the husband is presumed to be the father. Only the husband or wife may rebut this presumption by requesting blood tests within two years. Michael H., seeking to establish paternity, claimed that the California statute violated his due process rights.[148] The Court disagreed, recognizing no fundamental liberty that allows the plaintiff to assert visitation rights with his daughter against an intact family. Allowing him to make a claim of illegitimacy of a child may disrupt the integrity of the marital union.[149] The Court affirmed the judgment for the defendant husband.

In a famous footnote to this case, Justice Scalia, who wrote the opinion, criticized the dissent for its high level of generality in defining the rights in question. For Scalia, the Court must narrowly interpret the rights in question and "adopt the most specific tradition as the point of reference."[150] The question was not whether

---

[146] *Michael H. v. Gerald D.*, 491 U.S. 110 (1989).
[147] *Id.* at 114.
[148] *Id.* at 113.
[149] *Id.* at 131.
[150] *Id.* at 127.

the Constitution protects the right to parenthood; rather, it is whether a father has a fundamental right to the visitation of his children adulterously conceived. Scalia concluded that there is no such fundamental right based on the history and traditions of America and the Constitution.[151]

Thus, under *Michael H. v. Gerald D.*, states have the liberty to determine whether to allow paternity suits to be brought against a married couple. If a state refuses to do so by statute, the act would not be unconstitutional.

In the case of New Jersey, a rebuttable presumption that a man is the biological father of a child applies under certain circumstances, including the following:

- He attempts to marry the child's mother before the child's birth, but the marriage is invalid;
- The child is born while the woman and the man are married or within three hundred days of their divorce;
- The man welcomes the child into his home while the child is a minor and holds the child out as his own; or
- He acknowledges paternity in a writing that is filed with the local registrar and the mother does not dispute the writing.[152]

New Jersey, like California and several other states, allows the presumption of fatherhood to be rebutted when it arises because the man was married to the woman when the child was born. New Jersey law permits a third party to sue in order rebut the presumption and prove that he is the biological father of the child in question.[153] However, in weighing evidence, a court may only allow blood tests and genetic testing in determining if a man is the biological father of a child if the court determines with clear and convincing evidence that doing so will be in the best interests of the child.[154]

---

[151] *Id.* at 127.
[152] *Id.* § 9:17-43.a.
[153] *Id.* § 9:17-45.
[154] *M.F. v. N.H.*, 252 N.J.Super. 420, 599 A.2d 1297 (N.J. App. Div. 1991).

PATERNITY PROCEEDINGS UNDER THE PARENTAGE ACT

The New Jersey Parentage Act provides the procedures for establishing parent-child relationships. Once an action is commenced in order to determine the existence of a father-child relationship, a consent conference is held. If an agreement between the parties is not reached, the case will go to court and a recommendation will be made to either dismiss the action or have the alleged father acknowledge his paternity. If the parties accept the recommendation to dismiss the action, a judgment of dismissal will be entered; if the alleged father acknowledges his paternity, a Certificate of Parentage will be executed.[155] This Certificate is a document that may be executed by a man testifying that he is a child's father. Like a proof of adoption, the Certificate can be the basis for bringing an action in child support.[156]

However, if the parties do not agree to dismiss the action and the alleged father refuses to acknowledge paternity, the county welfare agency or the court will order the parties to undergo blood or genetic testing, unless good cause is shown. All other relevant evidence will also be considered in determining the identity of the biological parents.[157] The Probation Division may receive information relating to putative father and child support obligors through various means and agencies, including any paper deemed necessary for attaining information on the obligor's assets, tax information from the Division of Taxation, and state lottery payments from the Department of the Treasury.[158] At hearings or trials for determining fatherhood in contested paternity suits, when a party fails to appear, a default order establishing paternity is to be entered when proper notice is served on the absent party. This default order is to be determinative.[159]

---

[155] N.J. Rev. Stat. § 9:17-48.
[156] *Id.* § 9:17-41.
[157] *Id.* § 9:17-48.
[158] *Id.* § 2A:17-56.34.
[159] *Id.* § 9:17-52.1.

New Jersey's Putative Spouse Doctrine

A putative spouse is a person who believes in good faith to be validly married to another person but who is in ignorance of some fault in the marriage that renders the marriage void or voidable, and whose spouse is aware of this. Under New Jersey's putative-spouse doctrine, in order to protect the innocent spouse, a void or voidable marriage is treated as though it were valid. The doctrine treats the relationship as a *de facto* marriage that grants the putative spouse, through equity, normal marital rights, including:

- A cause of action against the employer of an alleged spouse in cases of wrongful death[160]; and
- The right to workmen's compensation to the spouse of a decedent husband or wife when the spouse believed in good faith that she was married and there was a marriage ceremony and a *de facto* marriage relationship unbroken over a period of years.[161]

Assisted Reproductive Technology

Many couples hope to have children and start a family. Yet for many, infertility prevents this hope from becoming reality. Assisted reproductive technology has brought the solution to many couples.

Varied definitions exist for assisted reproductive technology. Some definitions are limited to only those procedures in which both sperm and eggs are handled, thus excluding artificial insemination, where only sperm is handled.[162] For the purposes of this chapter, however, artificial reproduction technology will be used in a broader sense to refer to any procedure that aids human reproduction, including artificial insemination.

Many medical procedures supporting couples with fertility issues are available, most notably, surrogacy, *in vitro* fertilization, and, as already mentioned, artificial insemination.

---

[160] *Gershon v. Regency Diving Ctr., Inc.*, 845 A.2d 720 (N.J. Super. 2004).

[161] *Parkinson* v. J. & S. Tool Co., 313 A.2d 609, 611 (N.J. 1974).

[162] *See, e.g.*, "Assisted Reproductive Technology," Centers for Disease Control and Prevention, available at <http://www.cdc.gov/art>.

Surrogacy

A surrogate mother is one who helps a couple to have a child by carrying the child to term and then surrendering the child to the couple. There are two ways that a woman can become a surrogate mother: (i) through becoming artificially inseminated with the husband's sperm; or (ii) through transferring to her uterus an embryo conceived by the couple.

The New Jersey Supreme Court has held that a surrogacy agreement where a couple pays a surrogate mother to deliver a child is "illegal, perhaps criminal, and potentially degrading to women."[163] Today, surrogate mothers may not receive compensation for carrying the child and they may not be subject to a binding agreement to give up the child after birth. In the 1988 case *Matter of Baby M,*[164] the New Jersey Supreme Court unanimously agreed that a contract where an adoptive mother pays a surrogate mother to deliver a baby is void as against public policy. In *Baby M*, the defendant surrogate mother argued that the surrogacy contract that gave custody of the child to the plaintiff father was invalid because the contract did not permit her to voluntarily give up the child; she was left with no choice. The Court agreed, comparing the contract to the sale of babies, which is forbidden under New Jersey adoption law.[165] The Court held that a woman's giving up her child is not voluntary when she is being compelled to do so by a contract she previously signed. Parental rights may not be contractually alienated.

Thus, although surrogacy agreements are still permitted in New Jersey, agreements in which a surrogate mother is monetarily compensated for giving up her child are unenforceable in New Jersey's courts.

---

[163] *Matter of Baby M,* 537 A.2d 1227, 1234 (N.J. 1988).
[164] *Matter of Baby M,* 537 A.2d 1227 (N.J. 1988).
[165] *Id.* at 1247.

In Vitro Fertilization

In vitro fertilization is realized when an egg is fertilized with sperm in a laboratory environment and later implanted in the uterus for gestation. A couple may enter into an agreement with a sperm or egg donor in order to complete the process. Agreements for the use of cyropreserved embryos (those preserved by cooling to sub-zero temperatures) resulting from *in vitro* fertilization, like surrogacy agreements, are enforceable if they do not bind either party at the time of the destruction or use of the embryo.

The moral and ethical issues raised by *in vitro* fertilization continue to arise with respect to frozen preembryos. One side of the debate sees the preembryos as life and insists that they must be used or donated, not destroyed. The other side of the debate does not consider them to be human life, but rather, as potential human life, and believes that the interests of a potential child are outweighed by the rights of biological parents to choose not to procreate.

This question has been recently visited by the New Jersey Supreme Court, which held in favor of the party who wanted preembryos destroyed. In the 2001 case *J.B. v. M.B.*, a couple undergoing *in vitro* fertilization produced eleven preembryos, seven of which were preserved.[166] The couple then separated and the wife filed for divorce.[167] She expressed her wish for the preembryos to be destroyed, but the husband wanted them to be used or donated. The Court held that, because there was no contract as to the use of the preembryos, the interests of the parties had to be weighed. Here, the donation of the preembryos against the wife's will would imply the raising of her biological children by strangers, in violation of her right not to procreate. The discarding of the embryos, on the other hand, would not violate the husband's right to procreate, since he was capable of fathering other children. The Court thus ruled in the wife's favor, ordering the preembryos to be destroyed or preserved at the husband's expense. The Court

---

[166] *J.B. v. M.B.*, 783 A.2d 707, 710 (N.J. 2001).
[167] *Id.* at 710.

reasoned that, "[w]ith respect to preembryos, the scales ordinarily would tip in favor of the right not to procreate if the opposing party could become a parent through other reasonable means."[168]

Artificial Insemination

Artificial insemination is an assisted reproductive technology procedure where semen is inserted into a woman's vagina by an artificial means in place of sexual intercourse. Under New Jersey law, if a woman is artificially inseminated under the supervision of a licensed physician with the semen of a man who is not her husband, and her husband consents, her husband is treated as the biological father.[169] The man who donated sperm has no rights or duties with respect to the child unless he and the woman enter an agreement to the contrary.[170]

---

[168] *Id.* at 716.
[169] N.J. Rev. Stat. § 9:17-44a.
[170] *Id.* § 9:17-44b.

9

CHILDREN, CUSTODY, AND VISITATION

INTRODUCTION

General Overview

Custody battles can be among the most difficult and emotional of the consequences of divorce. Determining custody requires parents already under the stress of a divorce to determine which one will have legal control over the care and residence of their child or children. Courts must determine which parent will become the custodial parent and which will become the non-custodial parent with visitation rights.

When deciding on custody, courts are primarily concerned with the best interests of the child. Courts therefore do everything they can to lessen the emotional and psychological impact on the children. When the parents cannot agree on who should have custody, or if the parents come to an agreement but the court believes that the agreement is *not* in the best interests of the child, the court may establish custody and visitation of its own accord.[171]

In custody battles, the rights of both parents will have equal weight absent evidence of misconduct.[172] However, even with all other factors being equal, there is a presumption that "the child's well-being is better safeguarded in the hands of the mother."[173] This theory is commonly referred to as "the tender years doctrine." Although it has been challenged as violating equal protection and

---

[171] N.J. Rev. Stat. § 9:2-4.c to 4.f.
[172] *Id.* § 9:2-4.
[173] *Wojnarowicz v. Wojnarowicz*, 137 A.2d 618, 620 (N.J. Ch. Div. 1958).

statutory requirements that parents be given equal rights absent abuse or neglect,[174] the theory continues to hold sway in New Jersey custody actions.

According to the doctrine, children are best cared for when custody is given to the mother, since she is usually the primary caregiver who feeds, dresses, and cares for them during their tender years. This presumption may be rebutted by the father if he can prove that the mother is so physically or morally deficient that the child's welfare and best interests will not be served by awarding her custody.[175]

Courts may choose between several alternatives when awarding custody, including sole custody to one parent and joint and divided custody to both parents. In addition, temporary custody may be awarded in emergency situations, generally between when the couple separates and when a final divorce and custody order is granted. During that period, courts try to avoid making changes in temporary custody awards until final custody is awarded.

Sole custody is custody granted to one parent, with "appropriate parenting time," or "visitation," granted to the other parent.[176] Under this arrangement, the custodial parent alone holds all of the legal rights, privileges, and responsibilities relating to the child.

Joint (shared) custody, on the other hand, is custody granted to both parents. Under joint custody, the parents have joint rights, duties, and responsibilities over the child. It can be legal, physical, or both legal and physical and nature. Joint legal custody refers to a situation where the child lives with one of the parents but both parents share in the rights, duties, and responsibilities relating to the child. Joint physical custody refers to a situation where the child spends time living with both parents, alternating between

---

[174] N.J. Rev. Stat. § 9:2-4.

[175] *Id.*

[176] *Id.* § 9:2-4.b.

households. Joint and legal custody is a combination of both of these forms.

Courts rarely award joint physical custody, since it is presumed that the child's best interests are served when she lives with one parent and has visitation with the other. When joint custody is granted, one parent generally remains the primary caretaker, the other is awarded visitation rights, and both share in the duties and obligations related to child rearing. The parents will make decisions together regarding the child's health, education, and welfare.[177]

In deciding whether to award joint custody, courts consider several factors, including (i) the ability of the parents to agree and cooperate on issues relating to the child's upbringing and well-being; (ii) whether both parents are willing and able—physically and psychologically—to accept custody of the child; and (iii) the child's own preference, when she is sufficiently mature to make an intelligent decision.[178]

Other Arrangements

Courts may also award other custody arrangements when doing so is in the best interests of the child.[179] One example is divided custody, sometimes referred to as "shared custody." When divided custody is awarded, both parents have residential custody of the child and the child spends an equal amount of time in each home. Neither parent pays child support, but each has responsibility over the child while the child is living with him. For example, under a divided custody order, a mother may live with the child with full responsibility and control during summer vacations and fall semesters, with the father taking control and responsibility during winter vacations and spring semesters.

---

[177] *Id.* § 9:2-4.a.
[178] *Id.* § 9:2-4.c.
[179] *Id.* § 9:2-4.c.

CODIFICATION OF THE BEST INTERESTS OF THE CHILD

When deciding and modifying custody and visitation awards, courts look to the best interests of the child. The New Jersey Legislature has codified the factors used to determine these interests. Courts thus look to the child custody statute when determining to which parent custody should be granted. The statute lists the following factors, among others[180]:

- the interaction and relation of the child with her parents and siblings;
- the preference of the child when she is of sufficient maturity to make an intelligent decision;
- the safety of the child from abuse by either parent;
- the stability of the home environment;
- the proximity of the homes of the parents;
- the extent and quality of the time each parent spent with the child; and
- each parent's fitness.

Although they are not enumerated in the statute, other factors, such as the importance of keeping siblings together as a family, have also been considered by the courts.[181]

Perhaps the most controversial of factors that courts must wrestle with in awarding custody is race. The United States Supreme Court has not held that race cannot be a factor in custody determination when it is related to the best interests of the child. However, it has stated that race, on its own, cannot be dispositive. Using race as a dispositive factor would violate the Equal Protection Clause of the Fourteenth Amendment.

In *Palmore v. Sidoti*,[182] the defendant, a white mother, was awarded custody of her daughter after divorcing the child's father, the plaintiff of the case. When the defendant later married and lived with a black man, the white father sued for custody of the child. He argued that the mother's custody should be terminated because she

---

[180] *Id.* § 9:2-4c.

[181] *S.M. v. S.J.*, 143 N.J. Super. 379, 384, 363 A.2d 353, 356 (Ch. Div. 1976).

[182] *Palmore v. Sidoti*, 466 U.S. 429, 104 S. Ct. 1879 (1984).

was living with and married to a man of a different race. Although the Florida trial court found that there was no issue as to the mother's fitness as a parent, it awarded the father custody, focusing on the harm that the effects of residential prejudice would have on a child living in a racially mixed household, which the lower court referred to as the *"social stigmatization that is sure to come."*[183] When the case reached the U.S. Supreme Court, the decision was reversed. Even if racial prejudice has real effects on the child, the Court reasoned, such prejudice cannot be the basis for removing the child from her mother's household.[184] Doing so would be like upholding a law forbidding blacks from purchasing property in white neighborhoods in order to "promote the public peace by preventing race conflicts."[185] Such an act, like this one, is prohibited by the federal Constitution.

The key holding in *Palmore* is that even though protecting the best interests of the child is a compelling state interest, a suspect classification based on race should not be upheld. Although the best interests of the child are paramount in child custody determinations, the negative effects of racial prejudice—no matter how real—cannot justify denying an otherwise fit parent custody of her child.

Nonetheless, some courts continue to use race as a factor in determining the best interests of the child. They may do so only if it is being used as one in a pool of many other factors.

CUSTODY AND VISITATION RIGHTS OF THIRD PARTIES

Visitation Rights of Grandparents and Siblings

New Jersey passed its first grandparent visitation statute in 1972. In 1993, the Legislature adopted the statute's present form, which permits grandparents and siblings to obtain visitation rights by applying for an order for visitation. Before obtaining the order, they must prove by the preponderance of the evidence that their

---

[183] *Palmore*, 466 U.S. at 430-31, 104 S. Ct. at 1880.
[184] *Palmore*, 466 U.S. at 434, 104 S. Ct. at 1882-83.
[185] *Palmore*, 466 U.S. at 433-34, 104 S. Ct. at 1882.

visitation will be in the child's best interests.[186] Among the factors that a court will consider when deciding whether to permit visitation are as follow[187]:

- The relationship between the child, the applicant, and the parents;
- The time period that has elapsed since the child last had contact with the applicant;
- The effect of the visitation on the child's relationship with her parents or those with whom she is residing;
- Any abuse or neglect by the applicant, whether it be physical, sexual, or emotional; and
- The applicant's good faith.

A *prima facie* presumption will be made that granting visitation rights will be in the best interests of the child when the applicant was a full-time caregiver of the child in the past.[188]

In *Troxel v. Granville*,[189] the U.S. Supreme Court held that the Due Process Clause of the Fourteenth Amendment prohibits states from interfering with parents' fundamental right to make decisions in the upbringing and education of their children. Unless it is found that a parent is unfit, states normally have no reason to deny him custody of his children. In *Troxel*, grandparents sued for the right to visit their grandchildren, against the mother's opposition. The Court held that the Fifth and Fourteenth Amendments protect against government interference of fundamental rights,[190] and among these fundamental rights is the right of parents to the care, custody, and control of their children.[191] When parents are fit, there is a presumption that they act in the best interests of the children. Since the defendant was a fit parent, she had a right to control who could visit her children. In light of this presumption, as well as the fact that the defendant already allowed the grandparents limited

---

[186] N.J. Rev. Stat. § 9:2-7.1.a.

[187] *Id.* § 9:2-7.1.b.

[188] *Id.* § 9:2-7.1.c.

[189] *Troxel v. Granville*, 530 U.S. 57, 120 S. Ct. 2054 (2000).

[190] *Troxel*, 530 U.S. at 65, 120 S. Ct. at 2059.

[191] *Troxel*, 530 U.S. at 66, 120 S. Ct. at 2060.

visitation with her children, the judgment for the mother was affirmed.[192]

The *Troxel* decision declared the Washington grandparental visitation statute unconstitutional because it failed to sufficiently protect the fundamental rights of parents to make decisions in rearing and controlling their children. That decision has put into question New Jersey's grandparent visitation statute, which does not even mention parents' rights as a factor in determining the visitation rights of third parties. In *Moriarty v. Bradt*, a New Jersey trial court granted grandparents visitation of their grandchildren despite the plaintiff father's opposition. The father challenged the constitutionality of New Jersey's grandparent visitation statute as applied in the case, arguing that under *Troxel*, it failed to adequately protect his rights as a parent.[193] The New Jersey Supreme Court disagreed, holding that if appropriately interpreted, the statute was not unconstitutional. In order to pass constitutional requirements, the statute would require grandparents to show by a preponderance of the evidence that the denial of visitation would harm the child.[194] Thus, even if a parent opposed visitation, the grandparents could overcome this opposition by showing that such a denial would harm the child. Finding that the grandparents had met this burden, the Court held in their favor, reinstating the visitation ordered by the trial court.[195] The U.S. Supreme Court's denial of *certiorari* seems to indicate its agreement with *Moriarty's* reading of *Troxel*.

Third Party Custody Rights

Parental rights are not absolute and may be terminated. There are two approaches for determining when a parent's rights should be terminated and custody of the children delivered to a third party:

- *"Parental right" doctrine*. Custody of the child is determined by the biological parent, unless a finding of parental

---

[192] *Troxel*, 530 U.S. at 75, 120 S. Ct. at 2065.
[193] *Moriarty v. Bradt*, 177 N.J. 84, 94, 827 A.2d 203, 208 (2003).
[194] *Moriarty*, 177 N.J. at 117, 827 A.2d at 224.
[195] *Moriarty*, 177 N.J. at 122, 827 A.2d at 228.

unfitness, intentional abandonment, or gross neglect without prospects for change leads to the termination of the parental rights.[196]

- *"Best interests of the child" approach.* Custody of the child is determined by the best interests of the child, regardless of parental unfitness.

The rules may appear to be mutually exclusive, especially in light of *Hoy v. Willis*,[197] where the Court ordered that custody be returned to the biological mother. The foster parent, the child's aunt, appealed a decision. Although she made no showing of parental unfitness, she argued that the child's remaining with her was in the best interest of the child. The court held that no showing of parental unfitness was necessary when the best interests of the child were served by granting custody to a third party.

The two approaches may not, however, actually be mutually exclusive. Under the "parental right" doctrine, there is a presumption that the parents will act in the best interests of her child; under the "best interests of the child" doctrine, there is a presumption that, absent parental unfitness, custody with the parents will be in the best interests of the child. Thus, in both cases, when the best interests of the child are served by giving custody to a third party, the parental rights will be terminated and custody will be given to the third party.

Termination of Custody

In considering the termination of custody rights, a court may consider any of the following[198]:

- the surrendering of custody of the child;
- the death, mental incompetence, or abandonment of parental responsibilities of the child's parent; or

---

[196] *See Matter of Baby M,* 537 A.2d 1227, 1252 (N.J. 1988).
[197] *Hoy v. Willis,* 165 N.J. Super. 265 (App. Div. 1978).
[198] N.J. Rev. Stat. § 9:2-19.

- the willful and continuous neglect or failed discharge of custodial responsibilities by a guardian or custodian that has been appointed for the child.

CUSTODY AND VISITATION RIGHTS OF SEX-ASSAULT CONVICTS

Any person convicted of sexual assault, sexual contact, or endangering the welfare of a child is denied custody and visitation rights of minor children, including any offspring born as a result of a sexual assault, unless clear and convincing evidence shows that the child's best interests would be served through awarding the convict custody or visitation.[199] A conviction for sexual assault does not, however, waive a person's child support obligations. Furthermore, the parental rights are not automatically terminated, even though visitation and custody rights are denied.[200]

MODIFICATION OF CUSTODY AND VISITATION

Parental rights may be permanently and involuntarily terminated when there is a showing of parental unfitness, intentional abandonment, or gross negligence without any reasonable prospect of change.[201] In normal cases of determining custody (*e.g.*, in actions of divorce), the loss of custody, by contrast, is not permanent. Rather, it is subject to modification, which can change, replace, or supersede a previous child custody determination.[202] If family circumstances *change substantially*, a court may modify a custody order, whether sole, joint, divided, or even permanent custody was originally ordered.

An example of a change in circumstances that could justify a child custody modification is relocation. If one of the parents relocates and it affects the best interests of the child, a court may consider modifying a previous custody and visitation order. Some courts have also considered a custodial parent's sexual relations

---

[199] N.J. Rev. Stat. § 9:2-4.1.a to -4.1.b.
[200] *Id.* § 9:2-4.1.c.
[201] *Matter of Baby M,* 537 A.2d 1227, 1252 (N.J. 1988).
[202] N.J. Rev. Stat. § 2A:34-54.

with a third person when considering custody modifications. In an older New Jersey case, a court threatened to revoke a mother's custody award if she did not modify her "exceedingly indiscreet" conduct,[203] but the extent to which today's courts would consider sexual relationships with a third party as a factor is unclear.

INTERFERENCE WITH CUSTODY

The Uniform Child Custody Jurisdiction Act (1968) (UCCJA) is a model statute that sets standards for the determination of a child's home state. In accordance with a child's residence in and connections with a state, the UCCJA determines which state is to have jurisdiction over the child in custody matters. It is this state which is to issue custody decrees that other states must follow. By 1981, all fifty states had adopted the UCCJA.[204]

In 1997, the Uniform Child Custody Jurisdiction Act was replaced by the Uniform Child Custody Jurisdiction and Enforcement Act (UCCJEA), which in turn was adopted by New Jersey in 2004.[205] This new model statute provides uniform methods for expediting orders of interstate custody and visitation. The UCCJEA brings the 1968 UCCJA into conformity with the federal Parental Kidnapping Prevention Act (PKPA) and the federal Violence Against Women Act (VAWA), while clarifying standards for determining which state is to have jurisdiction over child custody cases. The new statute also establishes standards to be used in determining custody through codifying the best interests of the child.

The UCCJEA more effectively deals with cases of child custody interference by providing enforcement mechanisms for child

---

[203] *Carey v. Carey*, 4 N.J. Misc. 1, 3-4, 131 A. 103, 104 (N.J. Ch. 1925).
[204] The National Conference of Commissioners on Uniform State Laws, *Uniform State Law Helps Enforce Child Custody Orders*, Uniform Law Commissioners (2000), available at
<http://www.nccusl.org/Update/pressreleases/pr1-00-4.asp>.
[205] Uniform Child Custody Jurisdiction Enforcement Act, N.J. Rev. Stat. § 2A:34-53 to -95.

custody and visitation orders.[206] The statute helps to prevent or otherwise resolve situations where a non-custodial parent kidnaps a child, takes him to another state, and initiates custody proceedings or modification of a custody order from the other state. Before the law was passed, state courts would proceed as though they had jurisdiction. Under the statute, however, courts give full faith and credit to court orders and custody decisions of the child's home state, which has the closest contact with the child and affords him the most stability and continuity. It is defined as the state where the child resided over the last six months with a parent or a person acting as a parent immediately before the start of a custody action.[207] The home state is to have jurisdiction over custody proceedings, and its orders and custody decisions are to have full faith and credit in the several states. The statute criminalizes child abduction, provides assistance in relocating abducted children, and requires states to enforce out of state custody orders. In addition, in emergencies, sister states may make orders of their own accord by assuming temporary emergency jurisdiction.[208]

---

[206] The National Conference of Commissioners on Uniform State Laws, *Uniform State Law Helps Enforce Child Custody Orders.*
[207] N.J. Rev. Stat. § 2A:34-54.
[208] *Id.* § 2A:38-68.

10

CHILDREN AND CHILD SUPPORT

INTRODUCTION

In addition to alimony, equitable distribution, custody, and visitation, divorcing couples often must handle the issue of child support. Regardless of whether a couple was married, a non-custodial parent may be required to pay child support to a custodial parent. If the couple was married and is seeking a divorce, the custodial parent may file for a child support order against the non-custodial parent in the divorce action. If the couple had a child out of wedlock and the child is living with one parent, that parent may also file for child support against the other parent. If the non-custodial parent is required to pay child support, the obligation will continue until the child is "emancipated," which usually occurs when the child reaches eighteen years of age.

A custodial parent may also file for temporary child support against the non-custodial parent during the period between their separation and the final divorce decree. This is known as *temporary support* and may be modified upon entry of the final divorce order. Temporary support is typically taken directly from the wages of the non-custodial parent, unless the parties agree otherwise or the judge finds good cause to waive this default rule.

CHILD SUPPORT GUIDELINES AND SCHEME

Guidelines were established to provide the courts a framework to determine a fair and workable child support scheme.[209] These

---

[209] New Jersey Rules of Practice, Appendix IX-A.1.

guidelines for determining child support, unlike those for determining alimony and equitable distribution awards, are based on objective criteria. Child support awards are derived from factual data, including each spouse's gross income, tax withholding, mandatory retirement contributions, and child care costs. Determinations of child support thus involve much less judicial discretion than determinations of alimony and equitable distribution. The non-custodial parent can plug in his financial data into mathematical equations and determine the sums that the court will expect him to pay for child support. However, although the New Jersey Rules Governing the Courts of the State of New Jersey determine child support by mathematical formulae, the statutorily prescribed results serve only as rebuttable presumptions of what the child support should be. As further explained below, judges retain some discretion in modifying the awards and parents may ask the court to modify the results if they can show good cause.

The Child Support Guidelines of New Jersey, encoded in the New Jersey Court Rules, are to be used in determining each parent's share of child support. The party seeking support must submit a worksheet in accordance with Appendix IX of the Rules. If the party proposes an award that is different from the result established in the worksheet, the reasons must be stated and good cause must be shown.[210] When determining the amount of child support, courts look to the guidelines established in Appendix IX of the Rules.[211] These include, but are not limited to:

- Each party's gross income;
- Tax withholding;
- Mandatory retirement contributions;
- Alimony paid and received;
- Prior child support orders;

---

[210] N.J. Court Rule 5:6A.

[211] Courts are to look to the guidelines defined in section 3 of P.L.1998, c.1 (C.2A:17-56.52), which in turn refer to New Jersey Court Rule 5:6A, which states that the guidelines established in Appendix IX of the New Jersey Court Rules are to be followed by the courts in determining child support.

- Costs of daycare;
- The child's health care premiums; and
- Unreimbursed health care expenses.

Appendix IX states that the formula to be used by the judge in calculating child support establishes a rebuttable presumption of the amount of support to be paid. If the judge finds that the formula's result is harsh, he may, with good cause, choose to modify it or to not use it at all.[212] When the court does not follow the Rules, it may consider a scheme that determines child support based on various factors set forth in the New Jersey statutes,[213] in order to guarantee that payments are made to cover medical and possible educational expenses.[214] Some of the factors considered by the courts include the following[215]:

- The standard of living of each parent;
- The ability of each parent to pay child support (more particularly, the sources of income and assets of each parent);
- The age and health of the child and each parent;
- The earning ability of each parent;
- Responsibility of the parents for the court-ordered support of others; and
- Any other factors that the court's judgment deems relevant.[216]

CHILD SUPPORT MODIFICATION

If the court finds that the circumstances of the parties have changed since the original child support order, it may modify the order. A party seeking a child support modification must file a motion

---

[212] New Jersey Rules of Practice, Appendix IX-A.2.
[213] *Id.* IX-A.3.
[214] N.J. Rev. Stat. § 2A:34-23.
[215] *Id.* § 2A:34-23.a. Only those factors also used by the courts when determining the amount of alimony to be paid to a spouse or in dividing marital property through equitable distribution are listed here. For a more thorough account, *see infra.*, "Summary of Factors Considered by Courts."
[216] *Id.* § 9:17-53e.

showing the change in circumstances.[217] For example, the non-custodial parent may be permitted to pay less if he undergoes a pay decrease or has new dependants. Conversely, if the custodial parent has more children or experiences a pay decrease, or the non-custodial parent experiences a pay increase, the court may order an upward modification of child support.[218]

TERMINATION OF CHILD SUPPORT

The obligation to pay child support terminates when the child becomes emancipated. This can occur in several ways, most notably when the child reaches majority (age eighteen), graduates from college with concomitant discontinuance of further education, marries, or obtains full-time employment. However, some pending legislative bills may change this.[219] Child support can also be terminated by the death of the child or the death of the non-custodial parent. Finally, if the parental rights are terminated through, for example, adoption of the child, the child support obligations also come to an end.

Reaching majority does not automatically terminate a parent's obligation to pay child support. If, for example, the child suffers from a severe mental condition that renders the child dependent on the parent, the parent must continue to pay child support, regardless of the child's age. Under these circumstances, before terminating the parent's obligation to pay child support, the court must first find that the child "is relieved of the incapacity or is no longer financially dependent on the parent."[220]

---

[217] New Jersey Rules of Practice, Appendix IX-A.23.
[218] *Id.* IX-A.20.a.
[219] *See* David M. Gorenburg, "New Jersey Divorce FAQ's," *Divorcenet.com,* July 17, 2004, available at
<http://www.divorcenet.com/states/new_jersey/njfaq06>.
[220] N.J. Rev. Stat. § 2A:34-23.

11.

ADOPTION

INTRODUCTION

Adoption is the process of placing a child with non-biological parents not related by blood. It involves a legal proceeding that creates a new parent-child relationship. The adoptive parents are given all of the rights and responsibilities legally linked with parentage and the child is entitled to all of the rights belonging to a natural child of the adoptive parents. These rights include, for example, the right to inherit.

Any person may adopt in New Jersey, but if the adoptive parent is married, she must first obtain the consent of her spouse, unless the couple brings the adoption action jointly.[221] In addition, absent special approval by the court, the adoptive parent must be at least eighteen years old and at least ten years older than the child.[222]

Before a child may be adopted, the parental rights of the child's natural parents must be terminated. However, under some circumstances, the child may be adopted without this termination. For example, a stepparent may adopt a child without terminating the biological parents' parental rights if he is married to one of the biological parents. This demonstrates a public policy of protecting "the best interests of the child above rigid constructions of the term 'family.'"[223]

---

[221] N.J. Rev. Stat. § 9:3-43.a.
[222] *Id.* § 9:3-43.b.
[223] *In re Adoption of a Child by J.M.G.*, 632 A.2d 550, 553 (N.J. Super. Ct. Ch. Div. 1993).

Parental rights may be terminated in several ways, including by placing the child for adoption in an adoption agency or for private adoption. Furthermore, parental rights can be terminated by the Division of Youth and Family Services (DYFS) of the Department of Children and Families.[224] The DYFS must file a guardianship petition in the Family Part of the Chancery Division. It will do so on any of the following grounds[225]:

-   A conviction of the parents for abuse, abandonment, neglect, or cruelty;
-   A showing that termination of the parental rights serves the best interests of the child;
-   The failure of the parent for a period of one year to remedy conditions that led to the child's being removed and accepted by the Division of Youth and Family Services or placed with an authorized agency, despite the Division's reasonable efforts to keep the family together and the parent's ability to remedy the situation;
-   The parent's abandonment of the child; or
-   A finding that the parent committed murder, aggravated manslaughter or manslaughter of one of her children; or committed another of a series of serious crimes defined by the New Jersey statutes on care, custody, and guardianship.

TYPES OF ADOPTIONS AND PROCEDURES

The procedures for obtaining an adoption vary according to whether the adoptive parents are applying for adoption through the Division of Youth and Family Services (DYFS) or through a private agency. Some elements, such as the requirement that the biological parents terminate their parental rights, are common to both kinds of adoptions. The termination of parental rights may occur voluntarily, through a judicial order for neglect or unfitness, or by operation of law (*e.g.*, for rape of the child). Furthermore, for

---

[224] N.J. Rev. Stat. § 30:4C-15 *et seq.*
[225] *Id.* § 30:4C-15.

both kinds of adoptions, the court must grant approval to the adoptive parents. In evaluating the application for DYFS adoption, the court considers the home study conducted by the DYFS; for private agency adoptions, the court considers the complaint filed by the adoptive parents.

Division of Youth and Family Services Adoptions

To adopt through the DYFS, a child must first be placed with the DYFS by his parents. In placing a child with the DYFS, the parent gives up his or her parental rights. The agency must inform the parent that the surrender of rights is permanent and irrevocable, except at the discretion of the approved agency or by court order.[226]

After the child is placed with the DYFS, the adoptive parents must file a complaint in the Chancery Division, Family Part. If the adoption agency approves the adoption and the court finds it in the best interests of the child, the adoption will be granted.

Private Adoptions

In order to obtain a private adoption, adoptive parents must file a complaint in the Chancery Division, Family Part. The biological parents may object to the adoption, unless their parental rights have already been terminated. To terminate the biological parents' rights, the court must find that they are unfit and that there is no reasonable prospect of change. The evidentiary standard for proving parental unfitness is clear and convincing evidence.[227]

Several weeks after the complaint is filed, the court will hold adoption hearings and consider whether the biological parents'

---

[226] *Id.* § 9:3-41.

[227] *See Santosky v. Kramer*, 466 U.S. 429 (1984), where the plaintiff Commissioner to County Dept. of Social Services sued to terminate the defendants' parental rights because of the defendants' negligence. The defendants argued that the N.Y. Statute allowing for termination of parental rights based on a preponderance of the evidence standard was unconstitutional. The Court reversed the judgment for the plaintiff, holding that, because of society's great interest in preserving the biological ties between parents and children, the standard to be used must be at least *clear and convincing evidence*.

rights should be terminated and the adoptive parents should be approved. A final hearing is then scheduled and, unless the adoptive parent is a stepparent, the investigating adoption agency conducts a home study. Taking place in the months between the initial and final hearings, the home study permits the agency to make its recommendation to the court. If the agency does not recommend adoption, the child will be appointed a guardian to represent her interests at the hearing.

GUARDIANS AND GUARDIANS *AD LITEM*

Children in adoption proceedings are often represented by a guardian or guardian *ad litem*. A guardian *ad litem* may represent an infant or incompetent person in a particular legal matter and make decisions on his behalf, even if these decisions do not conform to the wishes of the infant or incompetent person. The guardian *ad litem* is usually appointed when a child has no guardian in a legal proceeding. Although the guardian *ad litem* is generally a parent, a court may appoint another person if the proper petition is filed.

Like guardians *ad litem*, guardians are not required to be attorneys in order to represent the child. The main difference between the two is that while a guardian may be appointed for all purposes, a guardian *ad litem* is appointed for a specific matter or law suit. A guardian thus has broader authority than a guardian *ad litem* and may make any decision on behalf of the child, including those that are financial and medical in nature, and he may administer property rights. The child becomes the guardian's ward and the guardian is given the powers and obligations of a parent.

ADOPTION BY HOMOSEXUAL CO-HABITANTS

As mentioned above, anyone may apply to adopt a child in New Jersey, provided only that, if he is married, his spouse consents or the couple brings the action jointly and the requisite age requirements are fulfilled.[228] Unmarried couples may file for

---

[228] N.J. Rev. Stat. § 9:3-43.a.

adoption, regardless of gender and sexual orientation.[229] Thus, an unmarried same-sex couple may apply to adopt a child just as a heterosexual couple could.

Prior to the final adoption hearing, as earlier mentioned, an investigation (home study) by the adoption agency is required in private adoptions. As mentioned above, the home study requirement is waived when the applicant is the stepparent. The New Jersey courts have interpreted "stepparent" to include not only the spouse of the child's biological parent, but also, same-sex cohabitants who substantially cared for and helped raise the child along with the child's biological parent. If the same-sex cohabitant applies for adoption, she will be afforded the same rights as any stepparent, and the home study requirement will be waived. This rule applies when the child is bonded to the parent in a loving relationship and the best interests of the child are served.[230]

OPEN ADOPTION

Open adoption is adoption where a biological mother, sometimes along with a biological father, chooses parents to adopt her child and may continue to have a relationship with contact or visitation with the child.[231] Despite this continued contact, the legal and moral ties between the biological parents and the child are severed. Open adoption is similar to closed adoption in this respect, but is different in that in closed adoption, the biological parents give up the child to an unknown adoptive parent or parents and do not continue to have contact with the child.[232]

The New Jersey courts have at times approved adoption arrangements with the characteristics of open adoption. The courts have raised the question of whether the continued welfare of children placed for adoption requires continued contact with the

---

[229] *In Re Adoption of Two Children by H.N.R.*, 285 N.J. Super. 1, 7, 666 A.2d 535, 538 (Ct. App. Div. 1995).
[230] *Id.*
[231] *Black's Law Dictionary*, "open adoption" (8th ed. 2004).
[232] *Black's Law Dictionary*, "closed adoption" (8th ed. 2004).

biological parents,[233] and have at times approved adoption with this continued contact. For example, in *Matter of Guardianship of R.O.M.C.*, the trial judge ordered an open adoption in which the biological mother and her children had continued contact after the termination of the mother's parental rights, given the agreement of the biological mother, the foster parents, and a psychologist that this continued contact would be in the best interests of the children.[234]

---

[233] *See, e.g., In re Guardianship of J.C.*, 129 N.J. 1, 26, 608 A.2d 1312, 1324 (N.J. 1992).

[234] *Matter of Guardianship of R.O.M.C.*, 243 N.J. Super. 631, 633, 581 A.2d 113, 114 (App. Div. 1990).

12.

FAMILY LAW AND THE U.S. CONSTITUTION

Although states may, for the most part, freely regulate familial institutions such as marriage and divorce, any statute passed by a state legislature must meet the minimum protections guaranteed by the U.S. Constitution. Thus, New Jersey, like every state, must pay heed to the constitutional cases outlined in the present postscript, which deal with the guarantees of due process and equal protection.

DUE PROCESS

Due process is comprised of two distinct rights: procedural due process and substantive due process.

Procedural Due Process

Procedural due process comprises the rights in any legal suit to notice and a hearing. The U.S. Supreme Court has particularly emphasized these rights in divorce proceedings. Notice requires a defendant to be timely informed of any proceedings against him, such that he is able to prepare an adequate defense.[235] In addition to notice, procedural due process requires hearing—the right to be heard and present one's defense before the court adjudicating a particular dispute.

---

[235] *See Maynard v. Hill*, 125 U.S. 190 (1888), where a wife was not given notice of her husband's divorce proceeding against her

Substantive Due Process

Overview

Substantive due process is not as well-defined as procedural due process. Because it comprises a set of unenumerated rights, there is much controversy as to the exact scope of the protections of substantive due process. There is, however, general agreement that rights falling under its umbrella must be rooted in the nation's history and longstanding traditions. According to some case law, such rights must also be clearly described, judicially or otherwise.

For guidance as to what is meant by the nation's "history and traditions," we can consider the case *Washington v. Glucksberg*,[236] where plaintiffs sought to strike down a Washington ban on assisted suicide on the basis that it was unconstitutional. The Court found that American history and traditions do not support assisted suicide and that U.S. laws have continued to condemn them. Due process protects only the right to refuse life-saving treatment. The Court refused to expand this right to include the right to assisted suicide. Furthermore, the ban was held to be justified in that it was interrelated with the state's interest in preventing assisted suicide from becoming voluntary or involuntary euthanasia, which can threaten the poor, the weak, and the vulnerable.

In U.S. constitutional case law, language relating to "liberty" and "freedom" is often linked to due process. For example, in *Meyer v. Nebraska*,[237] a criminal judgment was entered against the defendant for violating a statute prohibiting teaching in German or any foreign language before the eighth grade. The Supreme Court, in attempting to define the scope and meaning of "liberty" protected in the Fourteenth Amendment's Due Process Clause, stated that it encompasses "not merely freedom from bodily restraint, but also the right of the individual to contract, to engage in any of the common occupations of life, to acquire useful knowledge, to marry, establish a home and bring up children, to worship God according to the dictates of his own conscience, and

---

[236] *Washington v. Glucksberg*, 173 S.Ct. 2258 (1997).
[237] *Meyer v. Nebraska*, 262 U.S. 390 (1923).

generally to enjoy those privileges long recognized at common law as essential to the orderly pursuit of happiness by free men." The Court reversed the judgment as it was based on a statute that infringed on the Fourteenth Amendment's due process rights, specifically, the fundamental right of parents to direct the educational upbringing of their children.

The case *Pierce v. Society of Sisters*[238] affirmed the rights declared in *Meyer*. Here, the Society of Sisters, who ran a religious orphanage, opposed an Oregon law that required children to attend public schools. The Court held that parents, who nurture and care for their children, have a right to dictate their children's education in a way that is free from state interference. The law was struck down.

Freedoms not Guaranteed by Substantive Due Process

Not all freedoms fall under the umbrella of due process. When the state has a legitimate interest, it may limit some freedoms when the limitation is rationally related to the state's interest. For example, in *Prince v. Massachusetts*,[239] the defendant Prince was convicted of violating labor laws when she had her sons and niece selling magazines, including *The Watchtower* and *Consolation*, as part of activities with the Jehovah's Witnesses. She argued that her religious views obligated her to put the children to work and that the statute violates her due process. The Court held that the state has a legitimate interest in stopping child labor and that the conviction was to stand. This case thus limits *Meyer* and *Pierce*, while reaffirming the principles articulated in *Reynolds v. U.S.*,[240] where a Mormon was told that religious beliefs do not permit the violation of bigamy statutes.

However, when a right is fundamental, courts apply a test known as "strict scrutiny" in determining whether a particular limitation is legitimate. This test requires that any limitation be necessary in order to secure a compelling state interest.

---

[238] *Pierce v. Society of Sisters*, 268 U.S. 510 (1925).
[239] *Prince v. Massachusetts*, 321 U.S. 158 (1944).
[240] *Reynolds v. United States*, 98 U.S. 145 (1878).

For example, strict scrutiny will be applied to state limitations on the fundamental right to marriage. In *Zablocki v. Redhail*,[241] a Wisconsin statute prohibited an individual in arrears in child support payments from obtaining a marriage license. The appellee challenged the statute as an unconstitutional limitation on the fundamental right to marriage, since the state's interest in assuring that children not become dependant on the state was not sufficiently compelling. The Court agreed and affirmed judgment against the statute.

Privacy

The Court has held that the right to privacy, though never mentioned or referenced in the Constitution, is an unenumerated fundamental right deeply ingrained in longstanding traditions and history.

Early on, the Court held privacy to include the right to use contraception. In *Griswold v. Connecticut*,[242] a statute prohibited both the use of contraceptives as well as assistance to third parties in contraceptive use. Planned Parenthood and a defendant doctor were convicted under the statute for giving advice on using contraceptives. Ruling on an appeal of the convictions, the Court held that the statute violated the Fourteenth Amendment and reversed the judgments.

The reasoning in *Griswold* can be said to have led to even broader privacy rights, eventually leading to *Lawrence v. Texas*,[243] which overturned the right of states to criminalize sodomy, as stated in *Bowers v. Hardwick*.[244]

In *Bowers v. Hardwick*, two men engaged in mutual, consensual oral sex were charged with violation of a Georgia statute criminalizing sodomy (in this case, defined as both oral and anal copulation). The plaintiff Hardwick sued to challenge the constitutionality of the statute based on privacy, and the Court held

---

[241] *Zablocki v. Redhail*, 434 U.S. 374 (1978).
[242] *Griswold v. Connecticut*, 381 U.S. 149 (1965).
[243] *Lawrence v. Texas*, 123 S.Ct. 2472 (2003).
[244] *Bowers v. Hardwick*, 478 U.S. 186 (1986).

that the fact that two adults engage in an act in private does not place the act under the protection of constitutional privacy, nor does it exonerate them for having violated the criminal law. Judgment for the plaintiff was reversed.

This case was reversed nearly two decades later in *Lawrence v. Texas*, which expanded privacy rights to include the right to sodomy. In *Lawrence*, a Texas sodomy statute was challenged, and Justice Kennedy, writing for the Court, highlighted an "emerging awareness" reflected in the nation's laws and traditions in the past half century that "liberty gives substantial protection to adult persons in deciding how to conduct their private lives in matters pertaining to sex." Given these laws and traditions, statutes criminalizing sodomy were held to be unconstitutional.

Justice Scalia, in a forceful dissent, sharply criticized the inconsistency and flippancy of the Court, which less than a decade earlier in *Planned Parenthood of Southeastern Pennsylvania v. Casey*[245] invoked *stare decisis* in order to uphold *Roe v. Wade*, yet here, was so quick to abandon *stare decisis* and the principles of *Bowers* in order to reach the result it desired and extend the sphere of privacy.

EQUAL PROTECTION

Overview

The basic rule for equal protection requires that two similarly situated groups must be similarly treated; the state may not discriminate against either group. In *Skinner v. Oklahoma*,[246] a law allowed the state to sterilize criminals who committed certain crimes. However, the law did not apply to white-collar crimes, such as embezzlement. Because the statute discriminated arbitrarily, it was held unconstitutional.

Similarly, in *Loving v. Virginia*,[247] a white male who married a black female challenged a statute that banned interracial marriage

---

[245] *Planned Parenthood of Southeastern Pennsylvania v. Casey*, 505 U.S. 833 (1992).
[246] *Skinner v. Oklahoma*, 316 U.S. 535 (1942).
[247] *Loving v. Virginia*, 388 U.S. 1 (1967).

on the basis that it violated equal protection by prohibiting interracial marriage only involving a white partner. The Court agreed and struck down the statute, holding that it "cannot stand consistently with the Fourteenth Amendment." Since marriage is a fundamental right, restrictions on it should be strictly scrutinized.

Also, in *Eisenstadt v. Baird*,[248] the defendant professor at Boston University, was convicted for exhibiting contraceptive articles at a lecture and of handing out vaginal foam to a student, in violation of a statute that limited distribution of contraceptives to married people only. The defendant petitioned for a writ of *habeas corpus*, and the Court held that if distribution to married persons is not prohibited, then distribution to unmarried persons cannot be prohibited under equal protection. Judgment was given in favor of the defendant.

Limitations on Equal Protection

When the state has a strong countervailing interest, it may legitimately treat distinct groups differently without violating the Constitution when such treatment is rationally related to the state's interest.

In *Sosna v. Iowa*,[249] the plaintiff sought to divorce her husband and was denied her petition on the basis that she had not met Iowa's one-year residency requirement and her husband was not an Iowa citizen. She sued on the constitutionality of the statute and appealed up to the Supreme Court, arguing that the statute unjustly discriminated against Iowa non-residents. The Court found that the statute was based on legitimate state interests—avoiding a collateral attack by a non-resident spouse if a divorce is granted and assuring that the resident is committed to the state when deciding on matters as important as divorce. The statute was not therefore unconstitutional in treating non-Iowans differently, since it was rationally related to legitimate state interests.

---

[248] *Eisenstadt v. Baird*, 405 U.S. 438 (1972).
[249] *Sosna v. Iowa*, 419 U.S. 393 (1975).

A law that denies suffering people the right to assisted suicide is not unconstitutional, even if the state simultaneously allows those on life support to end their lives by removing the support. In *Vacco v. Quill*,[250] the plaintiffs asserted that New York's law banning assisted suicide unconstitutionally violated equal protection. The Court, reaffirming that equal protection requires similarly situated cases to be treated the same, held that this law did not target a specific class. The case was not about denying those seeking assisted suicide the right held by those who voluntarily removed life-sustaining treatment. Whereas the former is a question of suicide, in the latter, it is the illness itself that causes death. Therefore, the two classes are not similarly situated. Judgment was granted for the defendant: the statute did not violate equal protection.

---

[250] *Vacco v. Quill*, 173 S.Ct. 2293 (1997).

APPENDICES

SELECT CONSTITUTIONAL PROVISIONS

United States Constitution

Fifth Amendment - Liberty Interest, Due Process

No person shall be held to answer for a capital, or otherwise infamous crime, unless on a presentment or indictment of a Grand Jury, except in cases arising in the land or naval forces, or in the Militia, when in actual service in time of War or public danger; nor shall any person be subject for the same offence to be twice put in jeopardy of life or limb; nor shall be compelled in any criminal case to be a witness against himself, nor be deprived of life, liberty, or property, without due process of law; nor shall private property be taken for public use, without just compensation.

Fourteenth Amendment - Citizenship Rights

Section 1. All persons born or naturalized in the United States and subject to the jurisdiction thereof, are citizens of the United States and of the State wherein they reside. No State shall make or enforce any law which shall abridge the privileges or immunities of citizens of the United States; nor shall any State deprive any person of life, liberty, or property, without due process of law; nor deny to any person within its jurisdiction the equal protection of the laws.

…

Section 5. The Congress shall have power to enforce, by appropriate legislation, the provisions of this article.

New Jersey Constitution

Article 1 – Rights and Privileges

1. All persons are by nature free and independent, and have certain natural and unalienable rights, among which are those of enjoying and defending life and liberty, of acquiring, possessing, and protecting property, and of pursuing and obtaining safety and happiness.

2. a. All political power is inherent in the people. Government is instituted for the protection, security, and benefit of the people, and they have the right at all times to alter or reform the same, whenever the public good may require it.

Article VI – Judicial, Section III

1. The Superior Court shall consist of such number of judges as may be authorized by law, each of whom shall exercise the powers of the court subject to rules of the Supreme Court. The Superior Court shall at all times consist of at least two judges who shall be assigned to sit in each of the counties of this State, and who are resident therein at the time of appointment and reappointment.

2. The Superior Court shall have original general jurisdiction throughout the State in all causes.

3. The Superior Court shall be divided into an Appellate Division, a Law Division, and a Chancery Division, which shall include a family part. Each division shall have such other parts, consist of such number of judges, and hear such causes, as may be provided by rules of the Supreme Court. At least two judges of the Superior Court shall at all times be assigned to sit in each of the counties of the State, who at the time of their appointment and reappointment were residents of that county provided, however, that the number of judges required to reside in the county wherein they sit shall be at least equal in number to the number of judges of the county court sitting in each of the counties at the adoption of this amendment.

Child Abuse Prevention and Treatment Act

N.J.R.S. Title 9, Subtitle 3, Chapter 6: Abuse, Abandonment, Cruelty, and Neglect of a Child

9:6-8.83 Short title.

1. This act shall be known as and may be cited as the "Comprehensive Child Abuse Prevention and Treatment Act." L.1997,c.175,s.1.

9:6-8.84 Definitions relative to child abuse, neglect.

2. As used in this act:

"Board" means the Child Fatality and Near Fatality Review Board established under P.L.1997, c.175 (C.9:6-8.83 et al.).

"Child" means any person under the age of 18.

"Commissioner" means the Commissioner of Children and Families.

"Division" means the Division of Youth and Family Services in the Department of Children and Families.

"Near fatality" means a case in which a child is in serious or critical condition, as certified by a physician.

"Panel" means a citizen review panel as established under P.L.1997, c.175 (C.9:6-8.83 et al.).

"Parent or guardian" means a person defined pursuant to section 1 of P.L.1974, c.119 (C.9:6-8.21) who has the responsibility for the care, custody or control of a child or upon whom there is a legal duty for such care.

"Reasonable efforts" means attempts by an agency authorized by the Division of Youth and Family Services to assist the parents in remedying the circumstances and conditions that led to the placement of the child and in reinforcing the family structure, as defined in section 7 of P.L.1991, c.275 (C.30:4C-15.1).

"Sexual abuse" means contacts or actions between a child and a parent or caretaker for the purpose of sexual stimulation of either that person or another person. Sexual abuse includes:

a. the employment, use, persuasion, inducement, enticement or coercion of any child to engage in, or assist any other person to engage in, any sexually explicit conduct or simulation of such conduct;

b. sexual conduct including molestation, prostitution, other forms of sexual exploitation of children or incest; or

c. sexual penetration and sexual contact as defined in N.J.S.2C:14-1 and a prohibited sexual act as defined in N.J.S.2C:24-4.

"Significant bodily injury" means a temporary loss of the functioning of any bodily member or organ or temporary loss of any one of the five senses.

"Withholding of medically indicated treatment" means the failure to respond to a child's life-threatening conditions by providing treatment, including appropriate nutrition, hydration, and medication which, in the treating physician's reasonable judgment, will most likely be effective in ameliorating or correcting all such conditions. The term does not include the failure to provide treatment, other than appropriate nutrition, hydration, or medication to a child when, in the treating physician's reasonable medical judgment:

a. the child is chronically and irreversibly comatose;

b. the provision of such treatment would merely prolong dying, not be effective in ameliorating or correcting all of the child's life-threatening conditions, or otherwise be futile in terms of the survival of the child; or

c. the provision of such treatment would be virtually futile in terms of the survival of the child and the treatment itself under such circumstances would be inhumane.

L.1997, c.175, s.2; amended 1999, c.53, s.16; 2006, c.47, s.58.

9:6-8.85 Procedures for responding to reports of medical neglect.

3. The commissioner shall establish procedures for responding to the reporting of medical neglect, including instances of withholding of medically indicated treatment from disabled children with life-threatening conditions, to provide for: a. coordination and consultation with persons designated by and within appropriate health care facilities, and b. prompt notification by these persons of cases of suspected medical neglect, including withholding of medically indicated treatment from disabled children with life-threatening conditions.

L.1997,c.175,s.3.

9:6-8.86 Pursuit of legal remedies for medical care.

4. The division may pursue any legal remedies, including the initiation of legal proceedings in a court of competent jurisdiction, as may be necessary to: a. prevent the withholding of medically indicated treatment from disabled children with life-threatening conditions, or b. provide medical care or treatment for a child when such care or treatment is necessary to prevent or remedy serious harm to the child or to prevent the withholding of medically indicated treatment from disabled children with life-threatening conditions.
L.1997,c.175,s.4.

9:6-8.87 Exception to requirement to provide reasonable efforts to reunify child with parent.

5. In any case in which the division accepts a child in care or custody, including placement, the division shall not be required to provide reasonable efforts to reunify the child with a parent if an exception to the requirement to provide reasonable efforts has been established in accordance with section 25 of P.L.1999, c.53 (C.30:4C-11.3).
L.1997, c.175, s.5; amended L.1999,c.53,s.17.

9:6-8.88 Child Fatality and Near Fatality Review Board.

6. There is established the Child Fatality and Near Fatality Review Board. For the purposes of complying with the provisions of Article V, Section IV, paragraph 1 of the New Jersey Constitution, the board is established within the Department of Children and Families, but notwithstanding the establishment, the board shall be independent of any supervision or control by the department or any board or officer thereof.
The purpose of the board is to review fatalities and near fatalities of children in New Jersey in order to identify their causes, their relationship to governmental support systems, and methods of prevention. The board shall describe trends and patterns of child fatalities and near fatalities in New Jersey; identify risk factors and their prevalence in these populations of children; evaluate the responses of governmental systems to children in families who are considered to be at high risk and to offer recommendations for improvement in those responses; characterize risk groups in terms that are compatible with the development of public policy;

improve the sources of data collection by developing protocols for autopsies, death investigations, and complete recording of cause of death on the death certificate; and provide case consultation to individuals or agencies represented by the board.

L.1997, c.175, s.6; amended 2006, c.47, s.59.

9:6-8.89 Membership, terms of board members.

7. a. The board shall consist of 14 members as follows: the Commissioner of Children and Families, the Commissioner of Health and Senior Services, the Director of the Division of Youth and Family Services in the Department of Children and Families, the Attorney General, the Child Advocate and the Superintendent of State Police, or their designees, the State Medical Examiner, and the Chairperson or Executive Director of the New Jersey Task Force on Child Abuse and Neglect, who shall serve ex officio; and six public members appointed by the Governor, one of whom shall be a representative of the New Jersey Prosecutors' Association, one of whom shall be a Law Guardian, one of whom shall be a pediatrician with expertise in child abuse and neglect, one of whom shall be a psychologist with expertise in child abuse and neglect, one of whom shall be a social work educator with experience and expertise in the area of child abuse or a related field and one of whom shall have expertise in substance abuse.

b. The public members of the board shall serve for three-year terms. Of the public members first appointed, three shall serve for a period of two years, and three shall serve for a term of three years. They shall serve without compensation but shall be eligible for reimbursement for necessary and reasonable expenses incurred in the performance of their official duties and within the limits of funds appropriated for this purpose. Vacancies in the membership of the board shall be filled in the same manner as the original appointments were made.

c. The Governor shall appoint a public member to serve as chairperson of the board who shall be responsible for the coordination of all activities of the board and who shall provide the technical assistance needed to execute the duties of the board.

d. The board is entitled to call to its assistance and avail itself of the services of employees of any State, county or municipal department, board, bureau, commission or agency as it may require and as may be available for the purposes of reviewing a case pursuant to the provisions of P.L.1997, c.175 (C.9:6-8.83 et al.). The board may also seek the advice of experts, such as persons specializing in the fields of pediatric, radiological, neurological, psychiatric, orthopedic and forensic medicine; nursing; psychology; social work; education; law enforcement; family law; substance abuse; child advocacy or other related fields, if the facts of a case warrant additional expertise.

L.1997, c.175, s.7; amended 2005, c.155, s.108; 2006, c.47, s.60.

9:6-8.90 Duties of board.

8. The board shall:

a. Identify the fatalities of children due to unusual circumstances according to the following criteria:

(1) The cause of death is undetermined;

(2) Death where substance abuse may have been a contributing factor;

(3) Homicide, child abuse or neglect;

(4) Death where child abuse or neglect may have been a contributing factor;

(5) Malnutrition, dehydration, or medical neglect or failure to thrive;

(6) Sexual abuse;

(7) Head trauma, fractures or blunt force trauma without obvious innocent reason such as auto accidents;

(8) Suffocation or asphyxia;

(9) Burns without obvious innocent reason such as auto accident or house fire; and

(10) Suicide.

b. Identify fatalities and near fatalities among children whose family, currently or within the last 12 months, were receiving services from the division.

L.1997,c.175,s.8.

9:6-8.91 Determinations of board; composition of team; report.

9. a. The board shall determine which fatalities shall receive full review. The board may establish local or regional community-based teams to review information regarding children identified by the board. At least one team shall be designated to review information regarding child fatalities due to unusual circumstances. At least one team shall be designated to review

child fatalities and near fatalities identified pursuant to subsection b. of section 8 of P.L.1997, c.175 (C.9:6-8.90) as well as child fatalities where information available to the board indicates that child abuse or neglect may have been a contributing factor.

b. Each team shall include, at a minimum, a person experienced in prosecution, a person experienced in local law enforcement investigation, a medical examiner, a public health advocate, a physician, preferably a pediatrician, and a casework supervisor from a division field office. As necessary to perform its functions, each team may add additional members or seek the advice of experts in other fields if the facts of a case warrant additional expertise.

c. Each team shall submit to the board chairperson a report of its findings and recommendations based upon its review of information regarding each child fatality or near fatality.
L.1997,c.175,s.9.

9:6-8.92 Confidential master file.

10. a. The board shall record the name, age, date of birth, place of death or pronouncement of death, date and time of death, and circumstances surrounding the death in a confidential master file. Similar information shall be recorded for each near fatality reviewed by the board. The file shall serve as the minimum record of the case and shall be the only file that contains the name of the child and shall not be subject to discovery, but may be used by the chairperson of the board to refer an individual case, including the board's deliberations and conclusions, to the extent necessary for an appropriate agency to investigate or to provide services.

b. Except as provided in subsection a. of this section, the deliberations and conclusions of the board and of its teams, related to a specific case, shall be confidential. Summary records that are prepared by the board and the teams on each reported case shall be free of information that would identify the child.

c. The summary reports, deliberations and conclusions of the board or its teams shall not supersede or replace the conclusions or opinions of the agencies that contribute information from their own records.

d. The board shall review the reports submitted by each team and issue an annual report to the Governor and the Legislature which includes the number of cases reviewed and specific non-

identifying information regarding cases of particular significance. The board shall also include in the report recommendations for achieving better coordination and collaboration among State and local agencies and recommendations for system-wide improvements in services to prevent fatalities and near fatalities among children.
L.1997,c.175,s.10.

9:6-8.93 Subpoena, review of records.

11. a. The board may subpoena and review records that pertain to the child, except as provided in any statute, regulation or Executive Order relating to the confidentiality of criminal investigations and criminal investigative files. The records subject to subpoena and review shall include, but are not limited to, private medical and hospital records, school records, mental health records, and other records which may be deemed pertinent to the review process and necessary for the formulation of a conclusion by the board.

b. Records obtained by the board pursuant to subsection a. of this section shall not be subject to subpoena.

c. If, at the time of initial notification or during the subsequent review, the board has reasonable cause to believe that the death is the result of child abuse or neglect, or has reasonable cause to believe that the death is the result of an on-going hazard to other members of the household, then the board shall notify or shall verify that notification has been made to the county prosecutor of the county wherein the death occurred or was pronounced, and to the division.
L.1997,c.175,s.11.

9:6-8.94 Immunity from liability for civil damages.

12. A member of the board shall not be liable for any civil damages as a result of providing in good faith any reports, records, opinions or recommendations pursuant to P.L.1997, c.175 (C.9:6-8.83 et al.).
13.
14. L.1997,c.175,s.12.
15.
16. 9:6-8.95 Solicitation of grants, other funds.
17.

18. 13. The board may solicit and receive grants and other funds made available from a governmental, public, private, nonprofit, or for-profit agency, including funds made available under any federal or State law, regulation or program.

19.

20. L.1997,c.175,s.13.

21.

22. 9:6-8.96 Regulations by board.

23.

24. 14. The board shall adopt regulations pursuant to the "Administrative Procedure Act," P.L.1968, c.410 (C.52:14B-1 et seq.) concerning the operation of the board, procedures for conducting reviews of cases involving child fatalities and near fatalities, and other matters necessary to effectuate the purposes of this act.

25.

26. L.1997,c.175,s.14.

27.

28. 9:6-8.97 Citizen review panels.

15. a. The commissioner shall designate three citizen review panels for the purpose of examining the policies and procedures of State and local agencies and, as appropriate, specific cases, and evaluating the extent to which the agencies are effectively discharging their child protection responsibilities.

b. The commissioner may designate as panels for the purposes of P.L.1997, c.175 (C.9:6-8.83 et al.), one or more existing entities established under federal or State law, if such entities have the capacity to satisfy the requirements of this act.

c. Each panel shall be composed of volunteer members who are broadly representative of the community in which the panel is established, including members who have expertise in the prevention and treatment of child abuse and neglect.

d. Each panel shall meet not less than once every three months.

e. The members of the panels:

(1) shall not disclose to any person or government official any identifying information about a specific child protection case with respect to which the panel is provided information; and

(2) shall not make public other information unless authorized by State statute.

f. Each panel shall have access to information as necessary to carry out its functions. Each panel is entitled to call to its assistance and avail itself of the services of employees of any State, county or municipal department, board, bureau, commission or agency as it may require and as may be available for the purposes of effectuating the provisions of P.L.1997, c.175 (C.9:6-8.83 et al.). This subsection shall not be construed to permit access to information which may compromise the integrity of a division investigation or a civil or criminal investigation or judicial proceeding.

g. Each panel shall prepare and make available to the public on an annual basis, a report containing a summary of its activities.

h. A member of the panel shall not be liable for any civil damages as a result of providing, in good faith, a report, record, opinion or recommendation pursuant to P.L.1997, c.175 (C.9:6-8.83 et al..

i. A panel may receive grants and other funds made available from any governmental, public, private, nonprofit or for-profit agency, including funds made available under any federal or State law, regulation or program.

L.1997,c.175,s.15.

9:6-8.98 Rules, regulations by department.

19. The Department of Children and Families shall adopt rules and regulations pursuant to the "Administrative Procedure Act," P.L.1968, c.410 (C.52:14B-1 et seq.) to effectuate the purposes of this act.

L.1997, c.175, s.19; amended 2006, c.47, s.61.

9:6-8.99 Regional diagnostic and treatment centers for child abuse and neglect established.

1. The Commissioner of Children and Families shall establish four regional diagnostic and treatment centers for child abuse and neglect affiliated with medical teaching institutions in the State that meet the standards adopted by the commissioner, in consultation with the New Jersey Task Force on Child Abuse and Neglect. The regional centers shall be located in the northern, north central, south central and southern regions of the State. Each center shall have experience in addressing the medical and mental health diagnostic and treatment needs of abused and neglected children in the region in which it is located.

L.1998, c.19, s.1; amended 2006, c.47, s.62.

9:6-8.100 Function of center, staffing.

2. Each center shall demonstrate a multidisciplinary approach to identifying and responding to child abuse and neglect. The center staff shall include, at a minimum, a pediatrician, a consulting psychiatrist, a psychologist and a social worker who are trained to evaluate and treat children who have been abused or neglected and their families. Each center shall establish a liaison with the district office of the Division of Youth and Family Services in the Department of Children and Families and the prosecutor's office from the county in which the child who is undergoing evaluation and treatment resides. At least one member of the staff shall also have an appropriate professional credential or significant training and experience in the identification and treatment of substance abuse.

Each center shall develop an intake, referral and case tracking process which assists the division and prosecutor's office in assuring that child victims receive appropriate and timely diagnostic and treatment services.

L.1998, c.19, s.2; amended 2006, c.47, s.63.

9:6-8.101. Purpose of center

3. The regional centers shall: evaluate and treat child abuse and neglect; be resources for the region and develop additional resources within the region; provide training and consultative services; and be available for emergency phone consultation 24 hours a day. The centers shall also be a source for research and training for additional medical and mental health personnel dedicated to the identification and treatment of child abuse and neglect.

The regional center may charge a sliding scale fee for services provided under this act.

L.1998,c.19,s.3.

9:6-8.102 Services provided by staff of center.

4. Services provided by the center's staff shall include, but not be limited to:

a. Providing psychological and medical evaluation and treatment of the child, counseling for family members and substance abuse assessment and mental health and substance abuse counseling for the parents or guardians of the child;

b. Providing referral for appropriate social services and medical care;

c. Providing testimony regarding alleged child abuse or neglect at judicial proceedings;

d. Providing treatment recommendations for the child and mental health and substance abuse treatment recommendations for his family, and providing mental health and substance abuse treatment recommendations for persons convicted of child abuse or neglect;

e. Receiving referrals from the Department of Children and Families and the county prosecutor's office and assisting them in any investigation of child abuse or neglect;

f. Providing educational material and seminars on child abuse and neglect and the services the center provides to children, parents, teachers, law enforcement officials, the judiciary, attorneys and other citizens.

L.1998, c.19, s.4; amended 2004, c.130, s.35; amended 2006, c.47, s.64.

9:6-8.103. Safety of child undergoing treatment assured

5. The regional center shall ensure the safety of a child undergoing treatment while the child is at the regional center to the extent permitted by law. The appropriate law enforcement officials and protective services providers shall continue to ensure the safety of the child to the extent permitted by law.

L.1998,c.19,s.5.

9:6-8.104 Establishment, maintenance of county-based multidisciplinary teams; "child advocacy center" defined.

6. Regional centers shall act as a resource in the establishment and maintenance of county-based multidisciplinary teams which work in conjunction with the county prosecutor and the Department of Children and Families in the investigation of child abuse and neglect in the county in which the child who is undergoing evaluation and treatment resides. The Commissioner of Children and Families, in consultation with the New Jersey Task Force on Child Abuse and Neglect, shall establish standards for a county team. The county team shall consist of representatives of the

following disciplines: law enforcement; child protective services; mental health; substance abuse identification and treatment; and medicine; and, in those counties where a child advocacy center has been established, shall include a staff representative of a child advocacy center, all of whom have been trained to recognize child abuse and neglect. The county team shall provide: facilitation of the investigation, management and disposition of cases of criminal child abuse and neglect; referral services to the regional diagnostic center; appropriate referrals to medical and social service agencies; information regarding the identification and treatment of child abuse and neglect; and appropriate follow-up care for abused children and their families.

As used in this section, "child advocacy center" means a county-based center which meets the standards for a county team established by the commissioner pursuant to this section and demonstrates a multidisciplinary approach in providing comprehensive, culturally competent child abuse prevention, intervention and treatment services to children who are victims of child abuse or neglect.

L.1998, c.19, s.6; amended 2001, c.344; 2004, c.130, s.36; 2006, c.47, s.65.

9:6-8.106 Rules, regulations.

8. The Commissioner of Children and Families shall adopt rules and regulations pursuant to the "Administrative Procedure Act," P.L.1968, c.410 (C.52:14B-1 et seq.) necessary to effectuate the provisions of this act.

L.1998, c.19, s.8; amended 2006, c.47, s.66.

Domestic Partnership Act

Title 26, Chapter 8A: Domestic Partnerships

26:8A-1 Short title.

1. This act shall be known and may be cited as the "Domestic Partnership Act."
L.2003,c.246,s.1.

26:8A-2 Findings, declarations relative to domestic partners.

2. The Legislature finds and declares that:

a. There are a significant number of individuals in this State who choose to live together in important personal, emotional and economic committed relationships with another individual;

b. These familial relationships, which are known as domestic partnerships, assist the State by their establishment of a private network of support for the financial, physical and emotional health of their participants;

c. Because of the material and other support that these familial relationships provide to their participants, the Legislature believes that these mutually supportive relationships should be formally recognized by statute, and that certain rights and benefits should be made available to individuals participating in them, including: statutory protection against various forms of discrimination against domestic partners; certain visitation and decision-making rights in a health care setting; and certain tax-related benefits; and, in some cases, health and pension benefits that are provided in the same manner as for spouses;

d All persons in domestic partnerships should be entitled to certain rights and benefits that are accorded to married couples under the laws of New Jersey, including: statutory protection through the "Law Against Discrimination," P.L.1945, c.169 (C.10:5-1 et seq.) against various forms of discrimination based on domestic partnership status, such as employment, housing and credit discrimination; visitation rights for a hospitalized domestic partner and the right to make medical or legal decisions for an incapacitated partner; and an additional exemption from the personal income tax and the transfer inheritance tax on the same basis as a spouse. The need for all persons who are in domestic partnerships, regardless of their sex, to have access to these rights and benefits is paramount in view of their essential relationship to any reasonable conception of basic human dignity and autonomy, and the extent to which they will play an integral role in enabling these persons to enjoy their familial relationships as domestic partners and to cope with adversity when a medical emergency arises that affects a domestic partnership, as was painfully but graphically illustrated on a large scale in the aftermath of the tragic events that befell the people of our State and region on September 11, 2001;

e. The Legislature, however, discerns a clear and rational basis for making certain health and pension benefits available to dependent domestic partners only in the case of domestic partnerships in which both persons are of the same sex and are therefore unable to enter into a marriage with each other that is recognized by New Jersey law, unlike persons of the opposite sex who are in a domestic partnership but have the right to enter into a marriage that is recognized by State law and thereby have access to these health and pension benefits; and

f. Therefore, it is the public policy of this State to hereby establish and define the rights and responsibilities of domestic partners. L.2003,c.246,s.2.

26:8A-3 Definitions relative to domestic partners.

3. As used in sections 1 through 9 of P.L.2003, c.246 (C.26:8A-1 through C.26:8A-9) and in R.S.26:8-1 et seq.:

"Affidavit of Domestic Partnership" means an affidavit that sets forth each party's name and age, the parties' common mailing address, and a statement that, at the time the affidavit is signed, both parties meet the requirements of this act for entering into a domestic partnership and wish to enter into a domestic partnership with each other.

"Basic living expenses" means the cost of basic food and shelter, and any other cost, including, but not limited to, the cost of health care, if some or all of the cost is paid as a benefit because a person is another person's domestic partner.

"Certificate of Domestic Partnership" means a certificate that includes: the full names of the domestic partners, a statement that the two individuals are members of a registered domestic partnership recognized by the State of New Jersey, the date that the domestic partnership was entered into, and a statement that the partners are entitled to all the rights, privileges and responsibilities accorded to domestic partners under the law. The certificate shall bear the seal of the State of New Jersey.

"Commissioner" means the Commissioner of Health and Senior Services.

"Domestic partner" or "partner" means a person who is in a relationship that satisfies the definition of a domestic partnership as set forth in this act.

"Have a common residence" means that two persons share the same place to live in this State, or share the same place to live in another jurisdiction when at least one of the persons is a member of a State-administered retirement system, regardless of whether or not: the legal right to possess the place is in both of their names; one or both persons have additional places to live; or one person temporarily leaves the shared place of residence to reside elsewhere, on either a short-term or long-term basis, for reasons that include, but are not limited to, medical care, incarceration, education, a sabbatical or employment, but intends to return to the shared place of residence.

"Jointly responsible" means that each domestic partner agrees to provide for the other partner's basic living expenses if the other partner is unable to provide for himself.

"Notice of Rights and Obligations of Domestic Partners" means a form that advises domestic partners, or persons seeking to become domestic partners, of the procedural requirements for establishing, maintaining, and terminating a domestic partnership, and includes information about the rights and responsibilities of the partners.

L.2003,c.246,s.3

26:8A-4 Affidavit of Domestic Partnership; establishment, requirements.

4. a. Two persons who desire to become domestic partners and meet the requirements of subsection b. of this section may execute and file an Affidavit of Domestic Partnership with the local registrar upon payment of a fee, in an amount to be determined by the commissioner, which shall be deposited in the General Fund. Each person shall receive a copy of the affidavit marked "filed."

b. A domestic partnership shall be established when all of the following requirements are met:

(1) Both persons have a common residence and are otherwise jointly responsible for each other's common welfare as evidenced by joint financial arrangements or joint ownership of real or personal property, which shall be demonstrated by at least one of the following:

(a) a joint deed, mortgage agreement or lease;

(b) a joint bank account;

(c) designation of one of the persons as a primary beneficiary in the other person's will;

(d) designation of one of the persons as a primary beneficiary in the other person's life insurance policy or retirement plan; or

(e) joint ownership of a motor vehicle;

(2) Both persons agree to be jointly responsible for each other's basic living expenses during the domestic partnership;

(3) Neither person is in a marriage recognized by New Jersey law or a member of another domestic partnership;

(4) Neither person is related to the other by blood or affinity up to and including the fourth degree of consanguinity;

(5) Both persons are of the same sex and therefore unable to enter into a marriage with each other that is recognized by New Jersey law, except that two persons who are each 62 years of age or older and not of the same sex may establish a domestic partnership if they meet the requirements set forth in this section;

(6) Both persons have chosen to share each other's lives in a committed relationship of mutual caring;

(7) Both persons are at least 18 years of age;

(8) Both persons file jointly an Affidavit of Domestic Partnership; and

(9) Neither person has been a partner in a domestic partnership that was terminated less than 180 days prior to the filing of the current Affidavit of Domestic Partnership, except that this prohibition shall not apply if one of the partners died; and, in all cases in which a person registered a prior domestic partnership, the domestic partnership shall have been terminated in accordance with the provisions of section 10 of P.L.2003, c.246 (C.26:8A-10).

c. A person who executes an Affidavit of Domestic Partnership in violation of the provisions of subsection b. of this section shall be liable to a civil penalty in an amount not to exceed $1,000. The penalty shall be sued for and collected pursuant to the "Penalty Enforcement Law of 1999," P.L.1999, c.274 (C.2A:58-10 et seq.). L.2003,c.246,s.4.

26:8A-5 Notice of termination of domestic partnerships to third parties; requirements.

5. a. A former domestic partner who has given a copy of the Certificate of Domestic Partnership to any third party to qualify for any benefit or right and whose receipt of that benefit or enjoyment of that right has not otherwise terminated, shall, upon termination of the domestic partnership, give or send to the third party, at the last known address of the third party, written notification that the domestic partnership has been terminated. A

third party that suffers a loss as a result of failure by a domestic partner to provide this notice shall be entitled to seek recovery from the partner who was obligated to send the notice for any actual loss resulting thereby.

b. Failure to provide notice to a third party, as required pursuant to this section, shall not delay or prevent the termination of the domestic partnership.

L.2003,c.246,s.5.

26:8A-6 Obligations of domestic partners.

6. a. The obligations that two people have to each other as a result of creating a domestic partnership shall be limited to the provisions of this act, and those provisions shall not diminish any right granted under any other provision of law.

b. Upon the termination of a domestic partnership, the domestic partners, from that time forward, shall incur none of the obligations to each other as domestic partners that are created by this or any other act.

c. A domestic partnership, civil union or reciprocal beneficiary relationship entered into outside of this State, which is valid under the laws of the jurisdiction under which the partnership was created, shall be valid in this State.

d. Any health care or social services provider, employer, operator of a place of public accommodation, property owner or administrator, or other individual or entity may treat a person as a member of a domestic partnership, notwithstanding the absence of an Affidavit of Domestic Partnership filed pursuant to this act.

e. Domestic partners may modify the rights and obligations to each other that are granted by this act in any valid contract between themselves, except for the requirements for a domestic partnership as set forth in section 4 of P.L.2003, c.246 (C.26:8A-4).

f. Two adults who have not filed an Affidavit of Domestic Partnership shall be treated as domestic partners in an emergency medical situation for the purposes of allowing one adult to accompany the other adult who is ill or injured while the latter is being transported to a hospital, or to visit the other adult who is a hospital patient, on the same basis as a member of the latter's immediate family, if both persons, or one of the persons in the event that the other person is legally or medically incapacitated, advise the emergency care provider that the two persons have met the other requirements for establishing a domestic partnership as set forth in section 4 of P.L.2003, c.246 (C.26:8A-4); however, the provisions of this section shall not be construed to permit the two adults to be treated as domestic partners for any other purpose as provided in P.L.2003, c.246 (C.26:8A-1 et al.) prior to their having filed an Affidavit of Domestic Partnership.

g. A domestic partner shall not be liable for the debts of the other partner contracted before establishment of the domestic partnership, or contracted by the other partner in his own name during the domestic partnership. The partner who contracts for the debt in his own name shall be liable to be sued separately in his own name, and any property belonging to that partner shall be liable to satisfy that debt in the same manner as if the partner had not entered into a domestic partnership.

L.2003,c.246,s.6.

26:8A-7 Preparation of forms and notices.

7. a. The commissioner shall cause to be prepared, in such a manner as the commissioner determines appropriate:

(1) blank forms, in quadruplicate, of Affidavits of Domestic Partnership and Certificates of Domestic Partnership corresponding to the requirements of this act; and

(2) copies of the Notice of the Rights and Obligations of Domestic Partners.

b. The commissioner shall ensure that these forms and notices, along with such sections of the laws concerning domestic partnership and explanations thereof as the commissioner may deem useful to persons having duties to recognize domestic partners under those laws, are printed and supplied to each local registrar, and made available to the public upon request.

L.2003,c.246,s.7.

26:8A-8 Duties of local registrar.

8. a. The local registrar shall:

(1) stamp each completed Affidavit of Domestic Partnership received with the date of its receipt and the name of the registration district in which it is filed; and

(2) immediately provide two copies of the stamped Affidavit of Domestic Partnership to the person who files that document.

b. Upon the filing of an Affidavit of Domestic Partnership and payment of the appropriate filing fee, the local registrar shall immediately complete a Certificate of Domestic Partnership with the domestic partners' relevant information and the date that the domestic partnership was established. The local registrar shall then issue to the domestic partners two copies of the certificate and two copies of the Notice of the Rights and Obligations of Domestic Partners. Copies of the Certificate of Domestic Partnership shall be prepared and recorded in the local registrar's records and with the State registrar.

c. Each local registrar shall, on or before the 10th day of each calendar month, or sooner if requested by the Department of Health and Senior Services, transmit to the State registrar the original of all the Affidavits of Domestic Partnership and Certificates of Domestic Partnership received or prepared by the local registrar for the preceding month.

L.2003,c.246,s.8.

26:8A-9 Duties of State registrar.

9. The State registrar shall cause all Affidavits of Domestic Partnership and Certificates of Domestic Partnership received to be alphabetically indexed by the surname of one of the partners, and shall establish a cross-referencing system to allow the records to be identified by the surname of the second partner. The State registrar shall also cause to be transcribed or otherwise recorded from the certificates any of the vital facts appearing thereon as the commissioner may deem necessary or useful.

L.2003,c.246,s.9.

26:8A-10 Jurisdiction of Superior Court relative to termination of domestic partnerships.

10. a. (1) The Superior Court shall have jurisdiction over all proceedings relating to the termination of a domestic partnership established pursuant to section 4 of P.L.2003, c.246 (C.26:8A-4), including the division and distribution of jointly held property. The fees for filing an action or proceeding for the termination of a domestic partnership shall be the same as those for filing an action or proceeding for divorce pursuant to N.J.S.22A:2-12.

(2) The termination of a domestic partnership may be adjudged for the following causes:

(a) voluntary sexual intercourse between a person who is in a domestic partnership and an individual other than the person's domestic partner as defined in section 3 of P.L.2003, c.246 (C.26:8A-3);

(b) willful and continued desertion for a period of 12 or more consecutive months, which may be established by satisfactory proof that the parties have ceased to cohabit as domestic partners;

(c) extreme cruelty, which is defined as including any physical or mental cruelty that endangers the safety or health of the plaintiff or makes it improper or unreasonable to expect the plaintiff to continue to cohabit with the defendant; except that no complaint for termination shall be filed until after three months from the date of the last act of cruelty complained of in the complaint, but this provision shall not be held to apply to any counterclaim;

(d) separation, provided that the domestic partners have lived separate and apart in different habitations for a period of at least 18 or more consecutive months and there is no reasonable prospect of reconciliation; and provided further that, after the 18-month period, there shall be a presumption that there is no reasonable prospect of reconciliation;

(e) voluntarily induced addiction or habituation to any narcotic drug, as defined in the "New Jersey Controlled Dangerous Substances Act," P.L.1970, c. 226 (C.24:21-2) or the "Comprehensive Drug Reform Act of 1987," N.J.S.2C:35-1 et al., or habitual drunkenness for a period of 12 or more consecutive months subsequent to establishment of the domestic partnership and next preceding the filing of the complaint;

(f) institutionalization for mental illness for a period of 24 or more consecutive months subsequent to establishment of the domestic partnership and next preceding the filing of the complaint; or

(g) imprisonment of the defendant for 18 or more consecutive months after establishment of the domestic partnership, provided that where the action is not commenced until after the defendant's release, the parties have not resumed cohabitation following the imprisonment.

(3) In all such proceedings, the court shall in no event be required to effect an equitable distribution of property, either real or personal, which was legally and beneficially acquired by both domestic partners or either domestic partner during the domestic partnership.

(4) The court shall notify the State registrar of the termination of a domestic partnership pursuant to this subsection.

b. In the case of two persons who are each 62 years of age or older and not of the same sex and have established a domestic partnership pursuant to section 4 of P.L.2003, c.246 (C.26:8A-4), the domestic partnership shall be deemed terminated if the two persons enter into a marriage with each other that is recognized by New Jersey law .

c. The State registrar shall revise the records of domestic partnership provided for in section 9 of P.L.2003, c.246 (C.26:8A-9) to reflect the termination of a domestic partnership pursuant to this section.

L.2003,c.246,s.10.

26:8A-11 Applicability of act.

58. a. The provisions of sections 41 through 56, inclusive, of P.L.2003, c. 246 shall only apply in the case of two persons who are of the same sex and have established a domestic partnership pursuant to section 4 of P.L.2003, c.246 (C.26:8A-4).

b. Notwithstanding any other provisions of law to the contrary, the provisions of subsection a. of this section shall not be deemed to be an unlawful discrimination under the "Law Against Discrimination," P.L.1945, c.169 (C.10:5-1 et seq.).

L.2003,c.246,s.58.

26:8A-12 Rules, regulations; responsible agencies.

59. a. The Commissioner of Health and Senior Services, pursuant to the "Administrative Procedure Act," P.L.1968, c.410 (C.52:14B-1 et seq.), shall adopt rules and regulations to effectuate the purposes of sections 1 through 10 and 13 through 35 of this act.

b. The Commissioner of Banking and Insurance, pursuant to the "Administrative Procedure Act," P.L.1968, c.410 (C.52:14B-1 et seq.), shall adopt rules and regulations to effectuate the purposes of sections 47 through 52, 55 and 56 of this act.

c. The New Jersey Individual Health Coverage Program Board, pursuant to the "Administrative Procedure Act," P.L.1968, c.410 (C.52:14B-1 et seq.), shall adopt rules and regulations to effectuate the purposes of section 53 of this act.

d. The New Jersey Small Employer Health Benefits Program Board, pursuant to the "Administrative Procedure Act," P.L.1968,

c.410 (C.52:14B-1 et seq.), shall adopt rules and regulations to effectuate the purposes of section 54 of this act.
L.2003,c.246,s.59.

26:8A-13 Dependent health benefits for domestic partners continued after retirement from certain local public employment.

3. In cases where entities choose to provide dependent health benefits coverage to employees' domestic partners pursuant to section 1 of P.L.1979, c.391 (C.18A:16-12) or N.J.S.40A:10-16, such coverage shall continue during the employees' retirement under the provisions of sections 7 and 8 of P.L.1979, c.391 (C.18A:16-18 and C.18A:16-19), N.J.S. 40A:10-22 and N.J.S. 40A:10-23. Nothing in this section shall be construed to limit an entity's right to extend benefits to, or withdraw benefits from, an employee or dependents of an employee.
L.2005,c.334,s.3.

New Jersey Parentage Act

Title 9, Subtitle 4, Chapter 17: Bastardy Proceedings

9:17-38. Short Title

This act shall be known and may be cited as the "New Jersey Parentage Act."
L.1983, c. 17, s. 1.

9:17-39. Parent and child relationship defined

As used in this act, "parent and child relationship" means the legal relationship existing between a child and the child's natural or adoptive parents, incident to which the law confers or imposes rights, privileges, duties, and obligations. It includes the mother and child relationship and the father and child relationship.
L.1983, c. 17, s. 2.

9:17-40. Extent of parent and child relationship

The parent and child relationship extends equally to every child and to every parent, regardless of the marital status of the parents.
L.1983, c. 17, s. 3.

9:17-41 Establishment of parent-child relationship; termination of natural parental rights; action.

4. The parent and child relationship between a child and:

a. The natural mother, may be established by proof of her having given birth to the child, or under P.L.1983, c.17 (C.9:17-38 et seq.);

b. The natural father, may be established by proof that his paternity has been adjudicated under prior law; under the laws governing probate; by giving full faith and credit to a determination of paternity made by any other state or jurisdiction, whether established through voluntary acknowledgment or through judicial or administrative processes; by a Certificate of Parentage as provided in section 7 of P.L.1994, c.164 (C.26:8-28.1) that is executed by the father, including an unemancipated minor, prior to or after the birth of a child, and filed with the appropriate State agency; by a default judgment or order of the court; or by an order of the court based on a blood test or genetic test that meets or exceeds the specific threshold probability as set by subsection i. of section 11 of P.L.1983, c.17 (C.9:17-48) creating a rebuttable presumption of paternity.

In accordance with section 331 of Pub.L.104-193, a signed voluntary acknowledgment of paternity shall be considered a legal finding of paternity subject to the right of the signatory to rescind the acknowledgment within 60 days of the date of signing, or by the date of establishment of a support order to which the signatory is a party, whichever is earlier.

The adjudication of paternity shall only be voided upon a finding that there exists clear and convincing evidence of: fraud, duress or a material mistake of fact, with the burden of proof upon the challenger;

c. An adoptive parent, may be established by proof of adoption;

d. The natural mother or the natural father, may be terminated by an order of a court of competent jurisdiction in granting a judgment of adoption or as the result of an action to terminate parental rights;

e. The establishment of the parent and child relationship pursuant to subsections a., b., and c. of this section shall be the basis upon which an action for child support may be brought by a party and acted upon by the court without further evidentiary proceedings;

f. In any case in which the parties execute a Certificate of Parentage or a rebuttable presumption of paternity is created

through genetic testing, the presumption of paternity under
section 6 of P.L.1983, c.17 (C.9:17-43) shall not apply;

g. Pursuant to the provisions of section 331 of Pub.L.104-193, the
child and other parties in a contested paternity case shall submit
to a genetic test upon the request of one of the parties, unless that
person has good cause for refusal, if the request is supported by a
sworn statement by the requesting party:

(1) alleging paternity and setting forth the facts establishing a
reasonable possibility of the requisite sexual contact between the
parties; or

(2) denying paternity and setting forth the facts establishing a
reasonable possibility of the nonexistence of sexual contact
between the parties;

h. In a contested paternity case in which the State IV-D agency
requires or the court orders genetic testing, the State IV-D agency
shall:

(1) pay the costs of the genetic test and may recoup payment from
the alleged father whose paternity is established; and

(2) obtain additional testing if the initial test results are contested,
and upon the request and advance payment for the additional test
by the contestant.

L.1983,c.17,s.4; amended 1994, c.164, s.1; 1997, c.376, s.3; 1998, c.1,
s.38.

9:17-42. Closed court; confidentiality of records

Notwithstanding any other law concerning public hearings and
records, any action or proceeding held under this act shall be held
in closed court without admittance of any person other than those
necessary to the action or proceeding. All papers and records and
any information pertaining to an action or proceeding held under
this act which may reveal the identity of any party in an action,
other than the final judgment or the birth certificate, whether part
of the permanent record of the court or of a file with the State
registrar of vital statistics or elsewhere, are confidential and are
subject to inspection only upon consent of the court and all parties
to the action who are still living, or in exceptional cases only upon
an order of the court for compelling reason clearly and
convincingly shown.

L.1983, c. 17, s. 5.

9:17-43 Presumptions.

6. a. A man is presumed to be the biological father of a child if:

(1) He and the child's biological mother are or have been married to each other and the child is born during the marriage, or within 300 days after the marriage is terminated by death, annulment or divorce;

(2) Before the child's birth, he and the child's biological mother have attempted to marry each other by a marriage solemnized in apparent compliance with law, although the attempted marriage is or could be declared invalid, and:

(a) if the attempted marriage could be declared invalid only by a court, the child is born during the attempted marriage, or within 300 days after its termination by death, annulment or divorce; or

(b) if the attempted marriage is invalid without a court order, the child is born within 300 days after the termination of cohabitation;

(3) After the child's birth, he and the child's biological mother have married, or attempted to marry, each other by a marriage solemnized in apparent compliance with law, although the attempted marriage is or could be declared invalid, and:

(a) he has acknowledged his paternity of the child in writing filed with the local registrar of vital statistics;

(b) he has sought to have his name placed on the child's birth certificate as the child's father, pursuant to R.S.26:8-40; or

(c) he openly holds out the child as his natural child; or

(d) he is obligated to support the child under a written voluntary agreement or court order;

(4) While the child is under the age of majority, he receives the child into his home and openly holds out the child as his natural child;

(5) While the child is under the age of majority, he provides support for the child and openly holds out the child as his natural child; or

(6) He acknowledges his paternity of the child in a writing filed with the local registrar of vital statistics, which shall promptly inform the mother of the filing of the acknowledgment, and she does not dispute the acknowledgment within a reasonable time after being informed thereof, in a writing filed with the local registrar. If another man is presumed under this section to be the child's father, acknowledgment may be effected only with the written consent of the presumed father. Each attempted

acknowledgment, whether or not effective, shall be kept on file by the local registrar of vital statistics and shall enTitle the person who filed it to notice of all proceedings concerning parentage and adoption of the child, as provided in section 10 of P.L.1983, c.17 (C.9:17-47) and pursuant to section 9 of P.L.1977, c.367 (C.9:3-45).

b. A presumption under this section may be rebutted in an appropriate action only by clear and convincing evidence. If two or more presumptions arise which conflict with each other, the presumption which on the facts is founded on the weightier considerations of policy and logic controls. The presumption is rebutted by a court order terminating the presumed father's paternal rights or by establishing that another man is the child's biological or adoptive father.

c. Notwithstanding the provisions of this section to the contrary, in an action brought under this act against the legal representative or the estate of a deceased alleged father, the criteria in paragraphs (4) and (5) of subsection a. of this section shall not constitute presumptions but shall be considered by the court together with all of the evidence submitted. The decision of the court shall be based on a preponderance of the evidence.

d. In the absence of a presumption, the court shall decide whether the parent and child relationship exists, based upon a preponderance of the evidence.

e. There is a rebuttable presumption that a man has knowledge of his paternity and the birth of a child if he had sexual intercourse with the biological mother within 300 days of the child's birth. This presumption may be rebutted only by clear and convincing evidence in an appropriate action based on fraud, duress, or misrepresentation by the biological mother concerning the paternity or birth of the child. This claim of fraud, duress, or misrepresentation must be asserted prior to the finalization of the adoption.

L.1983, c.17, s.6; amended 1998, c.20, s.4.

9:17-44. Artificial insemination

a. If, under the supervision of a licensed physician and with the consent of her husband, a wife is inseminated artificially with semen donated by a man not her husband, the husband is treated in law as if he were the natural father of a child thereby conceived. The husband's consent shall be in writing and signed by him and his wife. The physician shall certify their signatures and the date of the insemination, upon forms provided by the Department of Health, and file the husband's consent with the State Department of Health, where it shall be kept confidential and in a sealed file. However, the physician's failure to do so shall not affect the father and child relationship. All papers and records pertaining to the insemination, whether part of the permanent record of a court or of a file held by the supervising physician or elsewhere, are subject to inspection only upon an order of the court for compelling reasons clearly and convincingly shown.

b. Unless the donor of semen and the woman have entered into a written contract to the contrary, the donor of semen provided to a licensed physician for use in artificial insemination of a woman other than the donor's wife is treated in law as if he were not the father of a child thereby conceived and shall have no rights or duties stemming from the conception of a child.

L.1983, c. 17, s. 7.

9:17-45 Action to determine existence of parent-child relationship.

8. a. A child, a legal representative of the child, the natural mother, the estate or legal representative of the mother, if the mother has died or is a minor, a man alleged or alleging himself to be the father, the estate or legal representative of the alleged father, if the alleged father has died or is a minor, the Division of Family Development in the Department of Human Services, or the county welfare agency, or any person with an interest recognized as justiciable by the court may bring or defend an action or be made a party to an action at any time for the purpose of determining the existence or nonexistence of the parent and child relationship.

b. No action shall be brought under P.L.1983, c.17 (C.9:17-38 et seq.) more than five years after the child attains the age of majority.

c. The death of the alleged father shall not cause abatement of any action to establish paternity, and an action to determine the existence or nonexistence of the parent and child relationship may be instituted or continued against the estate or the legal representative of the alleged father.

d. Regardless of its terms, an agreement, other than an agreement approved by the court in accordance with subsection c. of section 11 of P.L.1983, c.17 (C.9:17-48) between an alleged or presumed father and the mother of the child, shall not bar an action under this section.

e. If an action under this section is brought before the birth of the child, all proceedings shall be stayed until after the birth, except service of process and the taking of depositions to perpetuate testimony. The court may consider the issue of medical expenses and may order the alleged father to pay the reasonable expenses of the mother's pregnancy and postpartum disability. Bills for pregnancy, childbirth and genetic testing are admissible as evidence without requiring third party foundation testimony, and shall constitute prima facie evidence of the amounts incurred for such services or for testing on behalf of the child.

f. This section does not extend the time within which a right of inheritance or a right to succession may be asserted beyond the time provided by law relating to distribution and closing of decedents' estates or to the determination of heirship, or otherwise, or limit any time period for the determination of any claims arising under the laws governing probate, including the construction of wills and trust instruments.

L.1983,c.17,s.8; amended 1997, c.376, s.2; 1998, c.1, s.39.

9:17-46. Jurisdiction

9. a. The Superior Court shall have jurisdiction over an action brought under this act. The action shall be joined with an action for divorce, annulment, separate maintenance or support.

b. A person who has sexual intercourse in this State thereby submits to the jurisdiction of the courts of this State as to an action brought under this act with respect to a child who may have been conceived by that act of intercourse. In addition to any other method provided by law, personal jurisdiction may be acquired by service in accordance with the rules of the court.

c. The action may be brought in the county in which the child or the alleged father resides or is found or, if the father is deceased, in which proceedings for probate of his estate have been or could be commenced.

L.1983,c.17,s.9; amended 1991,c.91,s.211.

9:17-47. Parties; guardian ad litem

The child may be made a party to the action. If the child is a minor and is made a party, a guardian ad litem may be appointed by the

court to represent the child. The child's mother or father may not represent the child as guardian or otherwise. The court may appoint an attorney-at-law or an appropriate State agency as guardian ad litem for the child. The natural mother, each man presumed to be the father under section 6, each man alleged to be the natural father, any one whose name appears on the birth certificate, and anyone who has attempted to file an acknowledgment under section 6, whether or not effective to create a presumption of paternity, shall be made parties or, if not subject to the jurisdiction of the court, shall be given notice of the action in a manner prescribed by the court and an opportunity to be heard. The court may align the parties.
L.1983, c. 17, s. 10.

9:17-48 Consent conference; settlement; contested cases, testing; presumptions.

11. a. As soon as practicable after an action to declare the existence or nonexistence of the father and child relationship has been brought, a consent conference shall be held by the Superior Court, Chancery Division, Family Part intake service, the Probation Division or the county welfare agency. At the request of either party, the determination of paternity may be referred directly to the court in lieu of the consent process. A court appearance shall be scheduled in the event that a consent agreement cannot be reached.

b. On the basis of the information produced at the conference, an appropriate recommendation for settlement shall be made to the parties, which may include any of the following:

(1) That the action be dismissed with or without prejudice; or

(2) That the alleged father voluntarily acknowledge his paternity of the child.

c. If the parties accept a recommendation made in accordance with subsection b. of this section, which has been approved by the court, judgment shall be entered or a Certificate of Parentage shall be executed accordingly.

d. If a party refuses to accept a recommendation made under subsection b. of this section or the consent conference is terminated because it is unlikely that all parties would accept a recommendation pursuant to subsection b. of this section, and blood tests or genetic tests have not been taken, the county welfare agency shall require or the court shall order the child and the parties to submit to blood tests or genetic tests unless a party claims, and the county welfare agency or the court finds, good cause for not ordering the tests. The court may hear and decide motions to challenge a directive issued by the county welfare agency requiring a party to submit to blood or genetic tests. A genetic test shall be ordered upon the request of either party, if the request is supported by a sworn statement by the requesting party which alleges paternity and sets forth the facts establishing a reasonable possibility of the requisite sexual contact between the parties or denies paternity and sets forth the facts establishing a reasonable possibility of the nonexistence of sexual contact between the parties. If a party refuses to acknowledge paternity based upon the blood or genetic test results, the action shall be set for a hearing.

If the results of the blood test or genetic test indicate that the specific threshold probability, as set by subsection i. of this section to establish paternity has been met or exceeded, the results shall be received in evidence as a rebuttable presumption of paternity without requiring any additional foundation testimony or proof of authenticity or accuracy of the paternity testing or results. In actions based on allegations of fraud or inaccurate analysis, the court or the county welfare agency shall require that additional blood or genetic tests be scheduled within 10 days of the request and be performed by qualified experts. Additional blood or genetic tests shall be paid for in advance by the requesting party.

If a party objects to the results of the blood or genetic tests, the party shall make the objection to the appropriate agency, in writing, within 10 days of the consent conference or hearing.

e. The guardian ad litem may accept or refuse to accept a recommendation under this section.

f. (Deleted by amendment, P.L.1994, c.164).

g. No evidence, testimony or other disclosure from the consent conference shall be admitted as evidence in a civil action except by consent of the parties. However, blood tests or genetic tests ordered pursuant to subsection d. of this section shall be admitted as evidence.

h. The refusal to submit to a blood test or genetic test required pursuant to subsection d. of this section, or both, shall be admitted into evidence and shall give rise to the presumption that the results of the test would have been unfavorable to the interests of the party who refused to submit to the test. Refusal to submit to a blood test or genetic test, or both, is also subject to the contempt power of the court.

i. Blood test or genetic test results indicating a 95% or greater probability that the alleged father is the father of the child shall create a presumption of paternity which may be rebutted only by clear and convincing evidence that the results of the test are not reliable in that particular case.

j. If a party refuses to acknowledge paternity or does not appear at a consent conference conducted by the county welfare agency, the county welfare agency shall refer the matter to the court for adjudication. For purposes of establishing paternity, the blood or genetic test results shall be admitted into evidence at the hearing without the need for foundation testimony or other proof of authenticity or accuracy, unless an objection is made.

L.1983,c.17,s.11; amended 1991, c.91, s.212; 1994, c.164, s.2; 1997, c.376, s.4; 1998, c.1, s.40.

9:17-49 Civil action under act; trial by court.

12. a. An action under this act is a civil action governed by the Rules Governing the Courts of the State of New Jersey.

b. The trial shall be by the court without a jury.

L.1983,c.17,s.12; amended 1998, c. 1, s.46.

9:17-50. Witnesses; compelling to testify; immunity; contempt; physician's testimony; admissibility of evidence

a. The mother of the child and the alleged father are competent to testify and may be compelled to testify.

b. Upon refusal of any witness, including a party, to testify under oath or produce evidence, the court may order the witness to testify under oath and produce evidence concerning all relevant facts. If the refusal is upon the ground that the testimony or evidence might tend to incriminate the witness, the court, after notice to the prosecutor, may grant the witness immunity from all criminal liability on account of the testimony or evidence that the witness is required to produce. An order granting immunity bars prosecution of the witness for any offense shown in whole or in part by testimony or evidence the witness is required to produce, except for perjury committed in the testimony. The refusal of a witness who has been granted immunity to obey an order to testify or produce evidence is a civil contempt of the court.

c. Testimony of a physician concerning the medical circumstances of the pregnancy, and the condition and characteristics of the child upon birth is not privileged.

d. Testimony relating to sexual access to the mother by any man at any time other than the probable time of conception of the child is inadmissible in evidence, unless offered by the mother. Before testimony relating to sexual access to the mother by an unidentified man at the probable time of conception may be introduced, the court shall hold an in camera hearing to determine whether the evidence is sufficiently probative so that the interests of justice require its admission.

e. In an action against an alleged father, uncorroborated evidence offered by him with respect to a man who is not subject to the jurisdiction of the court concerning his sexual intercourse with the mother at or about the probable time of conception of the child is admissible in evidence only if the other man has undergone blood tests or genetic tests, the results of which do not exclude the possibility of his paternity of the child and which tests are made available to the court. A man who is identified and is subject to the jurisdiction of the court shall be made a party in the action.

L.1983, c. 17, s. 13.

9:17-52. Evidence relating to paternity

Evidence relating to paternity may include:

a. Evidence of sexual intercourse between the mother and alleged father at any possible time of conception;

b. An expert's opinion concerning the statistical probability of the alleged father's paternity, based upon the duration of the mother's pregnancy;

c. Genetic or blood tests, weighted in accordance with evidence, if available, of the statistical probability of the alleged father's paternity;

d. Medical or anthropological evidence relating to the alleged father's paternity of the child, based on tests performed by experts. If a man has been identified as a possible father of the child, the court may, and upon request of a party shall, require the child, the mother, and the man to submit to appropriate tests; and

e. All other evidence on behalf of any party, relevant to the issue of paternity of the child.

L.1983, c. 17, s. 15.

9:17-52.1. Default order, effect

6. A default order shall be entered in a contested paternity action upon a showing that proper notice has been served upon the party and the party has failed to appear at a hearing or trial; or has failed to respond to a notice or order that required a response within a specific period of time. A default order entered pursuant to this section shall be determinative for purposes of establishing the existence of paternity when proper notice has been served and a sworn statement by the mother indicating the parentage of the child has been executed.

L.1994,c.164,s.6.

9:17-53 Judgment, order of court, certificate of parentage, amendment of birth record; amount of support.

16. a. The judgment or order of the court or a Certificate of Parentage determining the existence or nonexistence of the parent and child relationship is determinative for all purposes.

b. If the judgment or order of the court is at variance with the child's birth certificate, the court shall order that an amendment to the original birth record be made under section 22 of P.L.1983, c.17 (C.9:17-59).

c. The judgment or order may contain any other provision directed against the appropriate party to the proceeding concerning the duty of support, the custody and guardianship of the child, parenting time privileges with the child, the furnishing of bond or other security for the payment of the judgment, the repayment of any public assistance grant, or any other matter in the best interests of the child. The judgment or order may direct the father to pay the reasonable expenses of the mother's pregnancy and postpartum disability, including repayment to an agency which provided public assistance funds for those expenses. Bills for pregnancy, childbirth and blood or genetic testing are admissible as evidence without requiring third party foundation testimony, and shall constitute prima facie evidence of the amounts incurred for these services or for testing on behalf of the child.

d. Support judgments or orders ordinarily shall be for periodic payments, which may vary in amount. In the best interests of the child, the purchase of an annuity may be ordered in lieu of periodic payments of support. The court may limit a parent's liability for past support of the child to the proportion of the expenses already incurred that the court deems just.

e. In determining the amount to be paid by a parent for support of the child and the period during which the duty of support is owed, the court shall apply the child support guidelines as defined in section 3 of P.L.1998, c.1 (C.2A:17-56.52). In cases in which the court finds that a deviation from these guidelines is appropriate, the court shall consider all relevant facts when determining the amount of support, including the:

(1) Needs of the child;

(2) Standard of living and economic circumstances of each parent;

(3) Income and assets of each parent, including any public assistance grant received by a parent;

(4) Earning ability of each parent, including educational background, training, employment skills, work experience, custodial responsibility for children and the length of time and cost for each parent to obtain training or experience for appropriate employment;

(5) Need and capacity of the child for education, including higher education;

(6) Age and health of the child and each parent;

(7) Income, assets and earning ability of the child;

(8) Responsibility of the parents for the support of others; and

(9) Debts and liabilities of each child and parent.

The factors set forth herein are not intended to be exhaustive. The court may consider such other factors as may be appropriate under the circumstances.

The obligation to pay support for a child who has not been emancipated by the court shall not terminate solely on the basis of the child's age if the child suffers from a severe mental or physical incapacity that causes the child to be financially dependent on a parent. The obligation to pay support for that child shall continue until the court finds that the child is relieved of the incapacity or is no longer financially dependent on the parent. However, in assessing the financial obligation of the parent, the court shall consider, in addition to the factors enumerated in this section, the child's eligibility for public benefits and services for people with disabilities and may make such orders, including an order involving the creation of a trust, as are necessary to promote the well-being of the child.

As used in this section "severe mental or physical incapacity" shall not include a child's abuse of, or addiction to, alcohol or controlled substances.

f. Upon a motion by a party, the court shall enter a temporary support order pending a judicial determination of parentage if there is clear and convincing evidence of paternity supported by blood or genetic test results or other evidence.

L.1983,c.17,s.16; amended 1997, c.299, s.11; 1998, c.1, s.41; 2005, c.171, s.3.

9:17-54. Costs and fees

The court may order reasonable fees of counsel, experts, and the child's guardian ad litem, and other costs of the action and pre-trial proceedings, including blood or genetic tests, to be paid by the parties in proportions and at times determined by the court.
L.1983, c. 17, s. 17.

9:17-55. Enforcing parties

a. If existence of the father and child relationship is declared, or paternity or a duty of support has been acknowledged or adjudicated under this act or under prior law, the obligation of the father may be enforced in the same or other proceedings by the mother, and child, the public agency that has furnished or may furnish the reasonable expenses of pregnancy, postpartum disability, education, support, medical expenses, or burial, or by any other person, including a private agency, to the extent that the mother, child, person or agency has furnished or is furnishing these expenses.

b. The court may order support payments to be made to the mother, the clerk of the court, the appropriate probation department, or a person, corporation, or agency designated to administer them for the benefit of the child, under the supervision of the court.

c. Willful failure to obey the judgment or order of the court is a civil contempt of the court.

L. 1983, c. 17, s. 18. Amended by L. 1985, c. 278, s. 10, eff. Oct. 1, 1985.

9:17-56. Continuing jurisdiction

The court has continuing jurisdiction to modify or revoke a judgment or order.

L.1983, c. 17, s. 19.

9:17-57. Parties

The child, the mother or personal representative of the child, the Division of Public Welfare in the Department of Human Services or the county welfare agency, the personal representative or a parent, if the mother has died or is a minor, a man alleged or alleging himself to be the father, the personal representative or a parent of the alleged father, if the alleged father has died or is a minor, or any person with an interest recognized as justiciable by the court may bring an action to determine the existence or nonexistence of a mother and child relationship. Insofar as practicable, the provisions of this act applicable to the father and child relationship apply.

L.1983, c. 17, s. 20.

9:17-58. Support agreement

a. Any agreement in writing to furnish support for a child, growing out of a supposed or alleged father and child relationship, does not require consideration and is enforceable according to its terms, subject to subsection d. of section 8.

b. In the best interests of the child or the mother, the court may, and upon the request of the person agreeing to furnish support shall, order the agreement to be kept in confidence and designate a person or agency to receive and disburse on behalf of the child all amounts paid in performance of the agreement.

L.1983, c. 17, s. 21.

9:17-59. Amended birth record

a. Upon order of a court of this State or upon request of a court of another state, the local registrar of vital statistics shall prepare an amended birth record consistent with the findings of the court.

b. The fact that the father and child relationship was declared after the child's birth shall not be ascertainable from the amended birth record, but the actual place and date of birth shall be shown.

c. The evidence upon which the amended birth record was made and the original birth certificate shall be kept in a sealed and confidential file and be subject to inspection only upon consent of the court and all interested persons, or in exceptional cases only upon an order of the court for compelling reasons clearly and convincingly shown.

L.1983, c. 17, s. 22.

Prevention of Domestic Violence Act of 1991

Title 2C, Subtitle 2, Chapter 25: Domestic Violence

2C:25-17. Short Title

1. This act shall be known and may be cited as the "Prevention of Domestic Violence Act of 1991."
L.1991,c.261,s.1.

2C:25-18. Findings, declarations

2. The Legislature finds and declares that domestic violence is a serious crime against society; that there are thousands of persons in this State who are regularly beaten, tortured and in some cases even killed by their spouses or cohabitants; that a significant number of women who are assaulted are pregnant; that victims of domestic violence come from all social and economic backgrounds and ethnic groups; that there is a positive correlation between spousal abuse and child abuse; and that children, even when they are not themselves physically assaulted, suffer deep and lasting emotional effects from exposure to domestic violence. It is therefore, the intent of the Legislature to assure the victims of domestic violence the maximum protection from abuse the law can provide.

The Legislature further finds and declares that the health and welfare of some of its most vulnerable citizens, the elderly and disabled, are at risk because of incidents of reported and unreported domestic violence, abuse and neglect which are known to include acts which victimize the elderly and disabled emotionally, psychologically, physically and financially; because of age, disabilities or infirmities, this group of citizens frequently must rely on the aid and support of others; while the institutionalized elderly are protected under P.L.1977, c.239 (C.52:27G-1 et seq.), elderly and disabled adults in noninstitutionalized or community settings may find themselves victimized by family members or others upon whom they feel compelled to depend.

The Legislature further finds and declares that violence against the elderly and disabled, including criminal neglect of the elderly and disabled under section 1 of P.L.1989, c.23 (C.2C:24-8), must be recognized and addressed on an equal basis as violence against spouses and children in order to fulfill our responsibility as a society to protect those who are less able to protect themselves.

The Legislature further finds and declares that even though many of the existing criminal statutes are applicable to acts of domestic violence, previous societal attitudes concerning domestic violence have affected the response of our law enforcement and judicial systems, resulting in these acts receiving different treatment from similar crimes when they occur in a domestic context. The Legislature finds that battered adults presently experience substantial difficulty in gaining access to protection from the judicial system, particularly due to that system's inability to generate a prompt response in an emergency situation.

It is the intent of the Legislature to stress that the primary duty of a law enforcement officer when responding to a domestic violence call is to enforce the laws allegedly violated and to protect the victim. Further, it is the responsibility of the courts to protect victims of violence that occurs in a family or family-like setting by providing access to both emergent and long-term civil and criminal remedies and sanctions, and by ordering those remedies and sanctions that are available to assure the safety of the victims and the public. To that end, the Legislature encourages the training of all police and judicial personnel in the procedures and enforcement of this act, and about the social and psychological context in which domestic violence occurs; and it further encourages the broad application of the remedies available under this act in the civil and criminal courts of this State. It is further intended that the official response to domestic violence shall communicate the attitude that violent behavior will not be excused or tolerated, and shall make clear the fact that the existing criminal laws and civil remedies created under this act will be enforced without regard to the fact that the violence grows out of a domestic situation.

L.1991,c.261,s.2.

2C:25-19. Definitions

3. As used in this act:

a. "Domestic violence" means the occurrence of one or more of the following acts inflicted upon a person protected under this act by an adult or an emancipated minor:

(1) Homicide N.J.S.2C:11-1 et seq.

(2) Assault N.J.S.2C:12-1

(3) Terroristic threats N.J.S.2C:12-3

(4) Kidnapping N.J.S.2C:13-1

(5) Criminal restraint N.J.S.2C:13-2

(6) False imprisonment N.J.S.2C:13-3

(7) Sexual assault N.J.S.2C:14-2

(8) Criminal sexual contact N.J.S.2C:14-3

(9) Lewdness N.J.S.2C:14-4

(10) Criminal mischief N.J.S.2C:17-3

(11) Burglary N.J.S.2C:18-2

(12) Criminal trespass N.J.S.2C:18-3

(13) Harassment N.J.S.2C:33-4

(14) Stalking P.L.1992, c.209 (C.2C:12-10)

When one or more of these acts is inflicted by an unemancipated minor upon a person protected under this act, the occurrence shall not constitute "domestic violence," but may be the basis for the filing of a petition or complaint pursuant to the provisions of section 11 of P.L.1982, c.77 (C.2A:4A-30).

b. "Law enforcement agency" means a department, division, bureau, commission, board or other authority of the State or of any political subdivision thereof which employs law enforcement officers.

c. "Law enforcement officer" means a person whose public duties include the power to act as an officer for the detection, apprehension, arrest and conviction of offenders against the laws of this State.

d. "Victim of domestic violence" means a person protected under this act and shall include any person who is 18 years of age or older or who is an emancipated minor and who has been subjected to domestic violence by a spouse, former spouse, or any other person who is a present or former household member. "Victim of domestic violence" also includes any person, regardless of age, who has been subjected to domestic violence by a person with whom the victim has a child in common, or with whom the victim anticipates having a child in common, if one of the parties is pregnant. "Victim of domestic violence" also includes any person who has been subjected to domestic violence by a person with whom the victim has had a dating relationship.

e. "Emancipated minor" means a person who is under 18 years of age but who has been married, has entered military service, has a child or is pregnant or has been previously declared by a court or an administrative agency to be emancipated.

L.1991,c.261,s.3; amended 1994,c.93,s.1; 1994,c.94,s.1.

2C:25-20 Development of training course; curriculum.

4. a. (1) The Division of Criminal Justice shall develop and approve a training course and curriculum on the handling, investigation and response procedures concerning reports of domestic violence and abuse and neglect of the elderly and disabled. This training course and curriculum shall be reviewed at least every two years and modified by the Division of Criminal Justice from time to time as need may require. The Division of Criminal Justice shall distribute the curriculum to all local police agencies.

(2) The Attorney General shall be responsible for ensuring that all law enforcement officers attend initial training within 90 days of appointment or transfer and annual inservice training of at least four hours as described in this section.

b. (1) The Administrative Office of the Courts shall develop and approve a training course and a curriculum on the handling, investigation and response procedures concerning allegations of domestic violence. This training course shall be reviewed at least every two years and modified by the Administrative Office of the Courts from time to time as need may require.

(2) The Administrative Director of the Courts shall be responsible for ensuring that all judges and judicial personnel attend initial training within 90 days of appointment or transfer and annual inservice training as described in this section.

(3) The Division of Criminal Justice and the Administrative Office of the Courts shall provide that all training on the handling of

domestic violence matters shall include information concerning the impact of domestic violence on society, the dynamics of domestic violence, the statutory and case law concerning domestic violence, the necessary elements of a protection order, policies and procedures as promulgated or ordered by the Attorney General or the Supreme Court, and the use of available community resources, support services, available sanctions and treatment options. Law enforcement agencies shall: (1) establish domestic crisis teams or participate in established domestic crisis teams, and (2) shall train individual officers in methods of dealing with domestic violence and neglect and abuse of the elderly and disabled. The teams may include social workers, clergy or other persons trained in counseling, crisis intervention or in the treatment of domestic violence and neglect and abuse of the elderly and disabled victims.

L.1991,c.261,s.4; amended 1994, c.93, s.2; 1999, c.289; 1999, c.433, s.1.

2C:25-21 Arrest of alleged attacker; seizure of weapons, etc.

5. a. When a person claims to be a victim of domestic violence, and where a law enforcement officer responding to the incident finds probable cause to believe that domestic violence has occurred, the law enforcement officer shall arrest the person who is alleged to be the person who subjected the victim to domestic violence and shall sign a criminal complaint if:

(1) The victim exhibits signs of injury caused by an act of domestic violence;

(2) A warrant is in effect;

(3) There is probable cause to believe that the person has violated N.J.S.2C:29-9, and there is probable cause to believe that the person has been served with the order alleged to have been violated. If the victim does not have a copy of a purported order, the officer may verify the existence of an order with the appropriate law enforcement agency; or

(4) There is probable cause to believe that a weapon as defined in N.J.S.2C:39-1 has been involved in the commission of an act of domestic violence.

b. A law enforcement officer may arrest a person; or may sign a criminal complaint against that person, or may do both, where there is probable cause to believe that an act of domestic violence has been committed, but where none of the conditions in subsection a. of this section applies.

c. (1) As used in this section, the word "exhibits" is to be liberally construed to mean any indication that a victim has suffered bodily injury, which shall include physical pain or any impairment of physical condition. Where the victim exhibits no visible sign of injury, but states that an injury has occurred, the officer should consider other relevant factors in determining whether there is probable cause to make an arrest.

(2) In determining which party in a domestic violence incident is the victim where both parties exhibit signs of injury, the officer should consider the comparative extent of the injuries, the history of domestic violence between the parties, if any, and any other relevant factors.

(3) No victim shall be denied relief or arrested or charged under this act with an offense because the victim used reasonable force in self defense against domestic violence by an attacker.

d. (1) In addition to a law enforcement officer's authority to seize any weapon that is contraband, evidence or an instrumentality of crime, a law enforcement officer who has probable cause to believe that an act of domestic violence has been committed shall:

(a) question persons present to determine whether there are weapons on the premises; and

(b) upon observing or learning that a weapon is present on the premises, seize any weapon that the officer reasonably believes would expose the victim to a risk of serious bodily injury. If a law enforcement officer seizes any firearm pursuant to this paragraph, the officer shall also seize any firearm purchaser identification card or permit to purchase a handgun issued to the person accused of the act of domestic violence.

(2) A law enforcement officer shall deliver all weapons, firearms purchaser identification cards and permits to purchase a handgun seized pursuant to this section to the county prosecutor and shall append an inventory of all seized items to the domestic violence report.

(3) Weapons seized in accordance with the "Prevention of Domestic Violence Act of 1991", P.L.1991,c.261(C.2C:25-17 et seq.) shall be returned to the owner except upon order of the Superior Court. The prosecutor who has possession of the seized weapons may, upon notice to the owner, petition a judge of the Family Part

of the Superior Court, Chancery Division, within 45 days of seizure, to obtain Title to the seized weapons, or to revoke any and all permits, licenses and other authorizations for the use, possession, or ownership of such weapons pursuant to the law governing such use, possession, or ownership, or may object to the return of the weapons on such grounds as are provided for the initial rejection or later revocation of the authorizations, or on the grounds that the owner is unfit or that the owner poses a threat to the public in general or a person or persons in particular.

A hearing shall be held and a record made thereof within 45 days of the notice provided above. No formal pleading and no filing fee shall be required as a preliminary to such hearing. The hearing shall be summary in nature. Appeals from the results of the hearing shall be to the Superior Court, Appellate Division, in accordance with the law.

If the prosecutor does not institute an action within 45 days of seizure, the seized weapons shall be returned to the owner.

After the hearing the court shall order the return of the firearms, weapons and any authorization papers relating to the seized weapons to the owner if the court determines the owner is not subject to any of the disabilities set forth in N.J.S.2C:58-3c. and finds that the complaint has been dismissed at the request of the complainant and the prosecutor determines that there is insufficient probable cause to indict; or if the defendant is found not guilty of the charges; or if the court determines that the domestic violence situation no longer exists. Nothing in this act shall impair the right of the State to retain evidence pending a criminal prosecution. Nor shall any provision of this act be construed to limit the authority of the State or a law enforcement officer to seize, retain or forfeit property pursuant to chapter 64 of Title 2C of the New Jersey Statutes.

If, after the hearing, the court determines that the weapons are not to be returned to the owner, the court may:

(a) With respect to weapons other than firearms, order the prosecutor to dispose of the weapons if the owner does not arrange for the transfer or sale of the weapons to an appropriate person within 60 days; or

(b) Order the revocation of the owner's firearms purchaser identification card or any permit, license or authorization, in which case the court shall order the owner to surrender any firearm seized and all other firearms possessed to the prosecutor and shall order the prosecutor to dispose of the firearms if the owner does not arrange for the sale of the firearms to a registered dealer of the firearms within 60 days; or

(c) Order such other relief as it may deem appropriate. When the court orders the weapons forfeited to the State or the prosecutor is required to dispose of the weapons, the prosecutor shall dispose of the property as provided in N.J.S.2C:64-6.

(4) A civil suit may be brought to enjoin a wrongful failure to return a seized firearm where the prosecutor refuses to return the weapon after receiving a written request to do so and notice of the owner's intent to bring a civil action pursuant to this section. Failure of the prosecutor to comply with the provisions of this act shall enTitle the prevailing party in the civil suit to reasonable costs, including attorney's fees, provided that the court finds that the prosecutor failed to act in good faith in retaining the seized weapon.

(5) No law enforcement officer or agency shall be held liable in any civil action brought by any person for failing to learn of, locate or seize a weapon pursuant to this act, or for returning a seized weapon to its owner.

L.1991,c.261,s.5; amended 2003, c.277, s.1.

2C:25-21.1 Rules, regulations concerning weapons prohibitions and domestic violence.

6. The Attorney General may adopt, pursuant to the "Administrative Procedure Act," P.L.1968, c.410 (C.52:14B-1 et seq.), rules and regulations necessary and appropriate to implement this act.

L.2003,c.277,s.6.

2C:25-22. Immunity from civil liability

6. A law enforcement officer or a member of a domestic crisis team or any person who, in good faith, reports a possible incident of domestic violence to the police shall not be held liable in any civil action brought by any party for an arrest based on probable cause, enforcement in good faith of a court order, or any other act or omission in good faith under this act.

L.1991,c.261,s.6; amended 1994,c.94,s.2.

2C:25-23. Dissemination of notice to victim of domestic violence

7. A law enforcement officer shall disseminate and explain to the victim the following notice, which shall be written in both English and Spanish:

"You have the right to go to court to get an order called a temporary restraining order, also called a TRO, which may protect you from more abuse by your attacker. The officer who handed you this card can tell you how to get a TRO.

The kinds of things a judge can order in a TRO may include:

(1) That your attacker is temporarily forbidden from entering the home you live in;

(2) That your attacker is temporarily forbidden from having contact with you or your relatives;

(3) That your attacker is temporarily forbidden from bothering you at work;

(4) That your attacker has to pay temporary child support or support for you;

(5) That you be given temporary custody of your children;

(6) That your attacker pay you back any money you have to spend for medical treatment or repairs because of the violence. There are other things the court can order, and the court clerk will explain the procedure to you and will help you fill out the papers for a TRO.

You also have the right to file a criminal complaint against your attacker. The police officer who gave you this paper will tell you how to file a criminal complaint.

On weekends, holidays and other times when the courts are closed, you still have a right to get a TRO. The police officer who gave you this paper can help you get in touch with a judge who can give you a TRO."

L.1991,c.261,s.7.

2C:25-24 Domestic violence offense reports.

8. a. It shall be the duty of a law enforcement officer who responds to a domestic violence call to complete a domestic violence offense report. All information contained in the domestic violence offense report shall be forwarded to the appropriate county bureau of identification and to the State bureau of records and identification in the Division of State Police in the Department of Law and Public Safety. A copy of the domestic violence offense report shall

be forwarded to the municipal court where the offense was committed unless the case has been transferred to the Superior Court.

b. The domestic violence offense report shall be on a form prescribed by the supervisor of the State bureau of records and identification which shall include, but not be limited to, the following information:

(1) The relationship of the parties;

(2) The sex of the parties;

(3) The time and date of the incident;

(4) The number of domestic violence calls investigated;

(5) Whether children were involved, or whether the alleged act of domestic violence had been committed in the presence of children;

(6) The type and extent of abuse;

(7) The number and type of weapons involved;

(8) The action taken by the law enforcement officer;

(9) The existence of any prior court orders issued pursuant to this act concerning the parties;

(10) The number of domestic violence calls alleging a violation of a domestic violence restraining order;

(11) The number of arrests for a violation of a domestic violence order; and

(12) Any other data that may be necessary for a complete analysis of all circumstances leading to the alleged incident of domestic violence.

c. It shall be the duty of the Superintendent of the State Police with the assistance of the Division of Systems and Communications in the Department of Law and Public Safety to compile and report annually to the Governor, the Legislature and the Advisory Council on Domestic Violence on the tabulated data from the domestic violence offense reports, classified by county
L.1991,c.261,s.8; amended 1999, c.119, s.2.

2C:25-25. *Criminal complaints; proceedings*

9. The court in a criminal complaint arising from a domestic violence incident:

a. Shall not dismiss any charge or delay disposition of a case because of concurrent dissolution of a marriage, other civil proceedings, or because the victim has left the residence to avoid further incidents of domestic violence;

b. Shall not require proof that either party is seeking a dissolution of a marriage prior to institution of criminal proceedings;

c. Shall waive any requirement that the victim's location be disclosed to any person.

L.1991,c.261,s.9.

2C:25-26 *Release of defendant before trial; conditions.*

10. a. When a defendant charged with a crime or offense involving domestic violence is released from custody before trial on bail or personal recognizance, the court authorizing the release may as a condition of release issue an order prohibiting the defendant from having any contact with the victim including, but not limited to, restraining the defendant from entering the victim's residence, place of employment or business, or school, and from harassing or stalking the victim or victim's relatives in any way. The court may enter an order prohibiting the defendant from possessing any firearm or other weapon enumerated in subsection r. of N.J.S.2C:39-1 and ordering the search for and seizure of any such weapon at any location where the judge has reasonable cause to believe the weapon is located. The judge shall state with specificity the reasons for and scope of the search and seizure authorized by the order.

b. The written court order releasing the defendant shall contain the court's directives specifically restricting the defendant's ability to have contact with the victim or the victim's friends, co-workers or relatives. The clerk of the court or other person designated by the court shall provide a copy of this order to the victim forthwith.

c. The victim's location shall remain confidential and shall not appear on any documents or records to which the defendant has access.

d. Before bail is set, the defendant's prior record shall be considered by the court. The court shall also conduct a search of the domestic violence central registry. Bail shall be set as soon as is feasible, but in all cases within 24 hours of arrest.

e. Once bail is set it shall not be reduced without prior notice to the county prosecutor and the victim. Bail shall not be reduced by a judge other than the judge who originally ordered bail, unless the reasons for the amount of the original bail are available to the judge who reduces the bail and are set forth in the record.

f. A victim shall not be prohibited from applying for, and a court shall not be prohibited from issuing, temporary restraints pursuant to this act because the victim has charged any person with commission of a criminal act.

L.1991,c.261,s.10; amended 1994, c.94, s.3; 1999, c.421, s.2.

2C:25-26.1. Notification of victim of release of defendant

1. Notwithstanding any other provision of law to the contrary, whenever a defendant charged with a crime or an offense involving domestic violence is released from custody the prosecuting agency shall notify the victim.

L.1994,c.137,s.1.

2C:25-27 Conditions of sentencing of defendant found guilty of domestic violence.

11. When a defendant is found guilty of a crime or offense involving domestic violence and a condition of sentence restricts the defendant's ability to have contact with the victim, that condition shall be recorded in an order of the court and a written copy of that order shall be provided to the victim by the clerk of the court or other person designated by the court. In addition to restricting a defendant's ability to have contact with the victim, the court may require the defendant to receive professional counseling from either a private source or a source appointed by the court, and if the court so orders, the court shall require the defendant to provide documentation of attendance at the professional counseling. In any case where the court order contains a requirement that the defendant receive professional counseling, no application by the defendant to dissolve the restraining order shall be granted unless, in addition to any other provisions required by law or conditions ordered by the court, the defendant has completed all required attendance at such counseling.

L.1991,c.261,s.11; amended 1999, c.236, s.1.

2C:25-28 Filing complaint alleging domestic violence in Family Part; proceedings.

12. a. A victim may file a complaint alleging the commission of an act of domestic violence with the Family Part of the Chancery Division of the Superior Court in conformity with the Rules of

Court. The court shall not dismiss any complaint or delay disposition of a case because the victim has left the residence to avoid further incidents of domestic violence. Filing a complaint pursuant to this section shall not prevent the filing of a criminal complaint for the same act.

On weekends, holidays and other times when the court is closed, a victim may file a complaint before a judge of the Family Part of the Chancery Division of the Superior Court or a municipal court judge who shall be assigned to accept complaints and issue emergency, ex parte relief in the form of temporary restraining orders pursuant to this act.

A plaintiff may apply for relief under this section in a court having jurisdiction over the place where the alleged act of domestic violence occurred, where the defendant resides, or where the plaintiff resides or is sheltered, and the court shall follow the same procedures applicable to other emergency applications. Criminal complaints filed pursuant to this act shall be investigated and prosecuted in the jurisdiction where the offense is alleged to have occurred. Contempt complaints filed pursuant to N.J.S.2C:29-9 shall be prosecuted in the county where the contempt is alleged to have been committed and a copy of the contempt complaint shall be forwarded to the court that issued the order alleged to have been violated.

b. The court shall waive any requirement that the petitioner's place of residence appear on the complaint.

c. The clerk of the court, or other person designated by the court, shall assist the parties in completing any forms necessary for the filing of a summons, complaint, answer or other pleading.

d. Summons and complaint forms shall be readily available at the clerk's office, at the municipal courts and at municipal and State police stations.

e. As soon as the domestic violence complaint is filed, both the victim and the abuser shall be advised of any programs or services available for advice and counseling.

f. A plaintiff may seek emergency, ex parte relief in the nature of a temporary restraining order. A municipal court judge or a judge of the Family Part of the Chancery Division of the Superior Court may enter an ex parte order when necessary to protect the life, health or well-being of a victim on whose behalf the relief is sought.

g. If it appears that the plaintiff is in danger of domestic violence, the judge shall, upon consideration of the plaintiff's domestic violence complaint, order emergency ex parte relief, in the nature of a temporary restraining order. A decision shall be made by the judge regarding the emergency relief forthwith.

h. A judge may issue a temporary restraining order upon sworn testimony or complaint of an applicant who is not physically present, pursuant to court rules, or by a person who represents a person who is physically or mentally incapable of filing personally. A temporary restraining order may be issued if the judge is satisfied that exigent circumstances exist sufficient to excuse the failure of the applicant to appear personally and that sufficient grounds for granting the application have been shown.

i. An order for emergency, ex parte relief shall be granted upon good cause shown and shall remain in effect until a judge of the Family Part issues a further order. Any temporary order hereunder is immediately appealable for a plenary hearing de novo not on the record before any judge of the Family Part of the county in which the plaintiff resides or is sheltered if that judge issued the temporary order or has access to the reasons for the issuance of the temporary order and sets forth in the record the reasons for the modification or dissolution. The denial of a temporary restraining order by a municipal court judge and subsequent administrative dismissal of the complaint shall not bar the victim from refiling a complaint in the Family Part based on the same incident and receiving an emergency, ex parte hearing de novo not on the record before a Family Part judge, and every denial of relief by a municipal court judge shall so state.

j. Emergency relief may include forbidding the defendant from returning to the scene of the domestic violence, forbidding the defendant from possessing any firearm or other weapon enumerated in subsection r. of N.J.S.2C:39-1, ordering the search for and seizure of any such weapon at any location where the judge has reasonable cause to believe the weapon is located and the seizure of any firearms purchaser identification card or permit to purchase a handgun issued to the defendant and any other appropriate relief. The judge shall state with specificity the reasons for and scope of the search and seizure authorized by the order. The provisions of this subsection prohibiting a defendant from possessing a firearm or other weapon shall not apply to any law enforcement officer while actually on duty, or to any member of the Armed Forces of the United States or member of the National Guard while actually on duty or traveling to or from an authorized place of duty.

k. The judge may permit the defendant to return to the scene of the domestic violence to pick up personal belongings and effects but shall, in the order granting relief, restrict the time and duration of such permission and provide for police supervision of such visit.

l. An order granting emergency relief, together with the complaint or complaints, shall immediately be forwarded to the appropriate law enforcement agency for service on the defendant, and to the police of the municipality in which the plaintiff resides or is sheltered, and shall immediately be served upon the defendant by the police, except that an order issued during regular court hours may be forwarded to the sheriff for immediate service upon the defendant in accordance with the Rules of Court. If personal service cannot be effected upon the defendant, the court may order other appropriate substituted service. At no time shall the plaintiff be asked or required to serve any order on the defendant.

m. (Deleted by amendment, P.L.1994, c.94.)

n. Notice of temporary restraining orders issued pursuant to this section shall be sent by the clerk of the court or other person designated by the court to the appropriate chiefs of police, members of the State Police and any other appropriate law enforcement agency or court.

o. (Deleted by amendment, P.L.1994, c.94.)

p. Any temporary or permanent restraining order issued pursuant to this act shall be in effect throughout the State, and shall be enforced by all law enforcement officers.

q. Prior to the issuance of any temporary or permanent restraining order issued pursuant to this section, the court shall order that a search be made of the domestic violence central registry with regard to the defendant's record.

L.1991,c.261,s.12; amended 1994, c.94, s.4; 1999, c.421, s.3; 2003, c.277, s.5.

2C:25-28.1. In-house restraining order prohibited

2. Notwithstanding any provision of P.L.1991, c.261 (C.2C:25-17 et seq.) to the contrary, no order issued by the Family Part of the

Chancery Division of the Superior Court pursuant to section 12 or section 13 of P.L.1991, c.261 (C.2C:25-28 or 2C:25-29) regarding emergency, temporary or final relief shall include an in-house restraining order which permits the victim and the defendant to occupy the same premises but limits the defendant's use of that premises.
L.1995,c.242,s.2.

2C:25-29 Hearing procedure; relief.

13. a. A hearing shall be held in the Family Part of the Chancery Division of the Superior Court within 10 days of the filing of a complaint pursuant to section 12 of P.L.1991, c.261 (C.2C:25-28) in the county where the ex parte restraints were ordered, unless good cause is shown for the hearing to be held elsewhere. A copy of the complaint shall be served on the defendant in conformity with the Rules of Court. If a criminal complaint arising out of the same incident which is the subject matter of a complaint brought under P.L.1981, c.426 (C.2C:25-1 et seq.) or P.L.1991, c.261 (C.2C:25-17 et seq.) has been filed, testimony given by the plaintiff or defendant in the domestic violence matter shall not be used in the simultaneous or subsequent criminal proceeding against the defendant, other than domestic violence contempt matters and where it would otherwise be admissible hearsay under the rules of evidence that govern where a party is unavailable. At the hearing the standard for proving the allegations in the complaint shall be by a preponderance of the evidence. The court shall consider but not be limited to the following factors:
(1) The previous history of domestic violence between the plaintiff and defendant, including threats, harassment and physical abuse;
(2) The existence of immediate danger to person or property;
(3) The financial circumstances of the plaintiff and defendant;
(4) The best interests of the victim and any child;
(5) In determining custody and parenting time the protection of the victim's safety; and
(6) The existence of a verifiable order of protection from another jurisdiction.
An order issued under this act shall only restrain or provide damages payable from a person against whom a complaint has been filed under this act and only after a finding or an admission is made that an act of domestic violence was committed by that

person. The issue of whether or not a violation of this act occurred, including an act of contempt under this act, shall not be subject to mediation or negotiation in any form. In addition, where a temporary or final order has been issued pursuant to this act, no party shall be ordered to participate in mediation on the issue of custody or parenting time.

b. In proceedings in which complaints for restraining orders have been filed, the court shall grant any relief necessary to prevent further abuse. In addition to any other provisions, any restraining order issued by the court shall bar the defendant from purchasing, owning, possessing or controlling a firearm and from receiving or retaining a firearms purchaser identification card or permit to purchase a handgun pursuant to N.J.S.2C:58-3 during the period in which the restraining order is in effect or two years whichever is greater, except that this provision shall not apply to any law enforcement officer while actually on duty, or to any member of the Armed Forces of the United States or member of the National Guard while actually on duty or traveling to or from an authorized place of duty. At the hearing the judge of the Family Part of the Chancery Division of the Superior Court may issue an order granting any or all of the following relief:

(1) An order restraining the defendant from subjecting the victim to domestic violence, as defined in this act.

(2) An order granting exclusive possession to the plaintiff of the residence or household regardless of whether the residence or household is jointly or solely owned by the parties or jointly or solely leased by the parties. This order shall not in any manner affect Title or interest to any real property held by either party or both jointly. If it is not possible for the victim to remain in the residence, the court may order the defendant to pay the victim's rent at a residence other than the one previously shared by the parties if the defendant is found to have a duty to support the victim and the victim requires alternative housing.

(3) An order providing for parenting time. The order shall protect the safety and well-being of the plaintiff and minor children and shall specify the place and frequency of parenting time. Parenting time arrangements shall not compromise any other remedy provided by the court by requiring or encouraging contact between the plaintiff and defendant. Orders for parenting time may include a designation of a place of parenting time away from

the plaintiff, the participation of a third party, or supervised parenting time.

(a) The court shall consider a request by a custodial parent who has been subjected to domestic violence by a person with parenting time rights to a child in the parent's custody for an investigation or evaluation by the appropriate agency to assess the risk of harm to the child prior to the entry of a parenting time order. Any denial of such a request must be on the record and shall only be made if the judge finds the request to be arbitrary or capricious.

(b) The court shall consider suspension of the parenting time order and hold an emergency hearing upon an application made by the plaintiff certifying under oath that the defendant's access to the child pursuant to the parenting time order has threatened the safety and well-being of the child.

(4) An order requiring the defendant to pay to the victim monetary compensation for losses suffered as a direct result of the act of domestic violence. The order may require the defendant to pay the victim directly, to reimburse the Victims of Crime Compensation Board for any and all compensation paid by the Victims of Crime Compensation Board directly to or on behalf of the victim, and may require that the defendant reimburse any parties that may have compensated the victim, as the court may determine. Compensatory losses shall include, but not be limited to, loss of earnings or other support, including child or spousal support, out-of-pocket losses for injuries sustained, cost of repair or replacement of real or personal property damaged or destroyed or taken by the defendant, cost of counseling for the victim, moving or other travel expenses, reasonable attorney's fees, court costs, and compensation for pain and suffering. Where appropriate, punitive damages may be awarded in addition to compensatory damages.

(5) An order requiring the defendant to receive professional domestic violence counseling from either a private source or a source appointed by the court and, in that event, requiring the defendant to provide the court at specified intervals with documentation of attendance at the professional counseling. The court may order the defendant to pay for the professional counseling. No application by the defendant to dissolve a final order which contains a requirement for attendance at professional

counseling pursuant to this paragraph shall be granted by the court unless, in addition to any other provisions required by law or conditions ordered by the court, the defendant has completed all required attendance at such counseling.

(6) An order restraining the defendant from entering the residence, property, school, or place of employment of the victim or of other family or household members of the victim and requiring the defendant to stay away from any specified place that is named in the order and is frequented regularly by the victim or other family or household members.

(7) An order restraining the defendant from making contact with the plaintiff or others, including an order forbidding the defendant from personally or through an agent initiating any communication likely to cause annoyance or alarm including, but not limited to, personal, written, or telephone contact with the victim or other family members, or their employers, employees, or fellow workers, or others with whom communication would be likely to cause annoyance or alarm to the victim.

(8) An order requiring that the defendant make or continue to make rent or mortgage payments on the residence occupied by the victim if the defendant is found to have a duty to support the victim or other dependent household members; provided that this issue has not been resolved or is not being litigated between the parties in another action.

(9) An order granting either party temporary possession of specified personal property, such as an automobile, checkbook, documentation of health insurance, an identification document, a key, and other personal effects.

(10) An order awarding emergency monetary relief, including emergency support for minor children, to the victim and other dependents, if any. An ongoing obligation of support shall be determined at a later date pursuant to applicable law.

(11) An order awarding temporary custody of a minor child. The court shall presume that the best interests of the child are served by an award of custody to the non-abusive parent.

(12) An order requiring that a law enforcement officer accompany either party to the residence or any shared business premises to supervise the removal of personal belongings in order to ensure the personal safety of the plaintiff when a restraining order has been issued. This order shall be restricted in duration.

(13) (Deleted by amendment, P.L.1995, c.242).

(14) An order granting any other appropriate relief for the plaintiff and dependent children, provided that the plaintiff consents to such relief, including relief requested by the plaintiff at the final hearing, whether or not the plaintiff requested such relief at the time of the granting of the initial emergency order.

(15) An order that requires that the defendant report to the intake unit of the Family Part of the Chancery Division of the Superior Court for monitoring of any other provision of the order.

(16) In addition to the order required by this subsection prohibiting the defendant from possessing any firearm, the court may also issue an order prohibiting the defendant from possessing any other weapon enumerated in subsection r. of N.J.S.2C:39-1 and ordering the search for and seizure of any firearm or other weapon at any location where the judge has reasonable cause to believe the weapon is located. The judge shall state with specificity the reasons for and scope of the search and seizure authorized by the order.

(17) An order prohibiting the defendant from stalking or following, or threatening to harm, to stalk or to follow, the complainant or any other person named in the order in a manner that, taken in the context of past actions of the defendant, would put the complainant in reasonable fear that the defendant would cause the death or injury of the complainant or any other person. Behavior prohibited under this act includes, but is not limited to, behavior prohibited under the provisions of P.L.1992, c.209 (C.2C:12-10).

(18) An order requiring the defendant to undergo a psychiatric evaluation.

c. Notice of orders issued pursuant to this section shall be sent by the clerk of the Family Part of the Chancery Division of the Superior Court or other person designated by the court to the appropriate chiefs of police, members of the State Police and any other appropriate law enforcement agency.

d. Upon good cause shown, any final order may be dissolved or modified upon application to the Family Part of the Chancery Division of the Superior Court, but only if the judge who dissolves or modifies the order is the same judge who entered the order, or has available a complete record of the hearing or hearings on which the order was based.

e. Prior to the issuance of any order pursuant to this section, the court shall order that a search be made of the domestic violence central registry.

L.1991,c.261,s.13; amended 1994, c.94, s.5; 1994, c.137, s.2; 1995, c.242, s.1; 1997, c.299, s.8; 1999, c.236, s.2; 1999, c.421, s.4; 2003, c.277, s.2.

2C:25-29.1 Civil penalty for certain domestic violence offenders.

1. In addition to any other disposition, any person found by the court in a final hearing pursuant to section 13 of P.L.1991, c.261 (C.2C:25-29) to have committed an act of domestic violence shall be ordered by the court to pay a civil penalty of at least $50, but not to exceed $500. In imposing this civil penalty, the court shall take into consideration the nature and degree of injury suffered by the victim. The court may waive the penalty in cases of extreme financial hardship.

L.2001,c.195,s.1.

2C:25-29.2 Collection, distribution of civil penalties collected.

2. All civil penalties imposed pursuant to section 1 of P.L.2001, c.195 (C.2C:25-29.1) shall be collected as provided by the Rules of Court. All moneys collected shall be forwarded to the Domestic Violence Victims' Fund established pursuant to section 3 of P.L.2001, c.195 (C.30:14-15).

L.2001,c.195,s.2.

2C:25-29.3 Rules of Court.

4. The Supreme Court may promulgate Rules of Court to effectuate the purposes of this act.

L.2001,c.195,s.4.

2C:25-29.4 Surcharge for domestic violence offender to fund grants.

50. In addition to any other penalty, fine or charge imposed pursuant to law, a person convicted of an act of domestic violence, as that term is defined by subsection a. of section 3 of P.L.1991, c.261 (C.2C:25-19), shall be subject to a surcharge in the amount of $100 payable to the Treasurer of the State of New Jersey for use by the Department of Human Services to fund grants for domestic violence prevention, training and assessment.

L.2002,c.34,s.50.

2C:25-30. Violations, penalties

14. Except as provided below, a violation by the defendant of an order issued pursuant to this act shall constitute an offense under subsection b. of N.J.S.2C:29-9 and each order shall so state. All contempt proceedings conducted pursuant to N.J.S.2C:29-9 involving domestic violence orders, other than those constituting indictable offenses, shall be heard by the Family Part of the Chancery Division of the Superior Court. All contempt proceedings brought pursuant to P.L.1991, c.261 (C.2C:25-17 et seq.) shall be subject to any rules or guidelines established by the Supreme Court to guarantee the prompt disposition of criminal matters. Additionally, and notwithstanding the term of imprisonment provided in N.J.S.2C:43-8, any person convicted of a second or subsequent nonindictable domestic violence contempt offense shall serve a minimum term of not less than 30 days. Orders entered pursuant to paragraphs (3), (4), (5), (8) and (9) of subsection b. of section 13 of this act shall be excluded from enforcement under subsection b. of N.J.S.2C:29-9; however, violations of these orders may be enforced in a civil or criminal action initiated by the plaintiff or by the court, on its own motion, pursuant to applicable court rules.

L.1991,c.261,s.14; amended 1994,c.93,s.3; 1994,c.94,s.6.

2C:25-31 Contempt, law enforcement procedures.

15. Where a law enforcement officer finds that there is probable cause that a defendant has committed contempt of an order entered pursuant to the provisions of P.L.1981, c.426 (C.2C:25-1 et seq.) or P.L.1991, c.261 (C.2C:25-17 et seq.), the defendant shall be arrested and taken into custody by a law enforcement officer. The law enforcement officer shall follow these procedures:

The law enforcement officer shall transport the defendant to the police station or such other place as the law enforcement officer shall determine is proper. The law enforcement officer shall:

a. Conduct a search of the domestic violence central registry and sign a complaint concerning the incident which gave rise to the contempt charge;

b. Telephone or communicate in person or by facsimile with the appropriate judge assigned pursuant to this act and request bail be set on the contempt charge;

c. If the defendant is unable to meet the bail set, take the necessary steps to insure that the defendant shall be incarcerated at police headquarters or at the county jail; and

d. During regular court hours, the defendant shall have bail set by a Superior Court judge that day. On weekends, holidays and other times when the court is closed, the officer shall arrange to have the clerk of the Family Part notified on the next working day of the new complaint, the amount of bail, the defendant's whereabouts and all other necessary details. In addition, if a municipal court judge set the bail, the arresting officer shall notify the clerk of that municipal court of this information.

L.1991,c.261,s.15; amended 1994, c.94, s.7; 1999, c.421, s.5.

2C:25-32. *Alleged contempt, complainant's procedure*

16. Where a person alleges that a defendant has committed contempt of an order entered pursuant to the provisions of P.L.1981, c.426 (C.2C:25-1 et seq.) or P.L.1991, c.261, but where a law enforcement officer has found that there is not probable cause sufficient to arrest the defendant, the law enforcement officer shall advise the complainant of the procedure for completing and signing a criminal complaint alleging a violation of N.J.S.2C:29-9. During regular court hours, the assistance of the clerk of the Family Part of the Chancery Division of the Superior Court shall be made available to such complainants. Nothing in this section shall be construed to prevent the court from granting any other emergency relief it deems necessary.

L.1991,c.261,s.16.

2C:25-33 *Records of applications for relief; reports; confidentiality; forms.*

17. a. The Administrative Office of the Courts shall, with the assistance of the Attorney General and the county prosecutors, maintain a uniform record of all applications for relief pursuant to sections 9, 10, 11, 12, and 13 of P.L.1991, c.261 (C.2C:25-25, C.2C:25-26, C.2C:25-27, C.2C:25-28, and C.2C:25-29). The record shall include the following information:

(1) The number of criminal and civil complaints filed in all municipal courts and the Superior Court;

(2) The sex of the parties;

(3) The relationship of the parties;

(4) The relief sought or the offense charged, or both;

(5) The nature of the relief granted or penalty imposed, or both, including, but not limited to, the following:

(a) custody;

(b) child support;

(c) the specific restraints ordered;

(d) any requirements or conditions imposed pursuant to paragraphs (1) through (18) of subsection b. of section 13 of P.L.1991, c.261 (C.2C:25-29), including but not limited to professional counseling or psychiatric evaluations;

(6) The effective date of each order issued; and

(7) In the case of a civil action in which no permanent restraints are entered, or in the case of a criminal matter that does not proceed to trial, the reason or reasons for the disposition.

It shall be the duty of the Director of the Administrative Office of the Courts to compile and report annually to the Governor, the Legislature and the Advisory Council on Domestic Violence on the data tabulated from the records of these orders.

All records maintained pursuant to this act shall be confidential and shall not be made available to any individual or institution except as otherwise provided by law.

b. In addition to the provisions of subsection a. of this section, the Administrative Office of the Courts shall, with the assistance of the Attorney General and the county prosecutors, create and maintain uniform forms to record sentencing, bail conditions and dismissals. The forms shall be used by the Superior Court and by every municipal court to record any order in a case brought pursuant to this act. Such recording shall include but not be limited to, the specific restraints ordered, any requirements or conditions imposed on the defendant, and any conditions of bail.

L.1991,c.261,s.17; amended 1994, c.94, s.8; 1999, c.119, s.1; 1999, c.421, s.6.

2C:25-34 Domestic violence restraining orders, central registry.

1. The Administrative Office of the Courts shall establish and maintain a central registry of all persons who have had domestic violence restraining orders entered against them, all persons who have been charged with a crime or offense involving domestic violence, and all persons who have been charged with a violation of a court order involving domestic violence. All records made

pursuant to this section shall be kept confidential and shall be released only to:

a. A public agency authorized to investigate a report of domestic violence;

b. A police or other law enforcement agency investigating a report of domestic violence, or conducting a background investigation involving a person's application for a firearm permit or employment as a police or law enforcement officer or for any other purpose authorized by law or the Supreme Court of the State of New Jersey;

c. A court, upon its finding that access to such records may be necessary for determination of an issue before the court;

d. A surrogate, in that person's official capacity as deputy clerk of the Superior Court, in order to prepare documents that may be necessary for a court to determine an issue in an adoption proceeding; or

e. The Division of Youth and Family Services in the Department of Children and Families when the division is conducting a background investigation involving:

(1) an allegation of child abuse or neglect, to include any adult member of the same household as the individual who is the subject of the abuse or neglect allegation; or

(2) an out-of-home placement for a child being placed by the Division of Youth and Family Services, to include any adult member of the prospective placement household.

Any individual, agency, surrogate or court which receives from the Administrative Office of the Courts the records referred to in this section shall keep such records and reports, or parts thereof, confidential and shall not disseminate or disclose such records and reports, or parts thereof; provided that nothing in this section shall prohibit a receiving individual, agency, surrogate or court from disclosing records and reports, or parts thereof, in a manner consistent with and in furtherance of the purpose for which the records and reports or parts thereof were received.

Any individual who disseminates or discloses a record or report, or parts thereof, of the central registry, for a purpose other than investigating a report of domestic violence, conducting a background investigation involving a person's application for a firearm permit or employment as a police or law enforcement officer, making a determination of an issue before the court,

conducting a background investigation as specified in subsection e. of this section, or for any other purpose other than that which is authorized by law or the Supreme Court of the State of New Jersey, shall be guilty of a crime of the fourth degree.
L.1999, c.421, s.1; amended 2003, c.286, s.1; 2006, c.47, s.26.

2C:25-35 Rules of Court concerning central registry for domestic violence.

7. The Supreme Court of New Jersey may adopt Rules of Court appropriate or necessary to effectuate the purposes of this act.
L.1999,c.421,s.7.

Uniform Child Custody Jurisdiction and Enforcement Act

Title 2A, Subtitle 6, Chapter 34: Actions for Divorce or Nullity of Marriage

2A:34-53 Short title.

1. Short Title.
This act shall be known and may be cited as the "Uniform Child Custody Jurisdiction and Enforcement Act."
L.2004,c.147,s.1.

2A:34-54 Definitions.

2. Definitions.
As used in this act:
"Abandoned" means left without provision for reasonable and necessary care or supervision.
"Child" means an individual who has not attained 18 years of age.
"Child custody determination" means a judgment, decree, or other order of a court providing for the legal custody, physical custody or visitation with respect to a child. The term includes a permanent, temporary, initial and modification order. The term does not include a provision relating to child support or other monetary obligation of an individual.
"Child custody proceeding" means a proceeding in which legal custody, physical custody or visitation with respect to a child is an issue. The term includes a proceeding for divorce, separation, neglect, abuse, dependency, guardianship, paternity, termination of parental rights, and protection from domestic violence, in which the issue may appear. The term does not include a

proceeding involving juvenile delinquency, contractual emancipation or enforcement under article 3 of this act.

"Commencement" means the filing of the first pleading in a proceeding.

"Court" means an entity authorized under the law of a state to establish, enforce or modify a child custody determination.

"Home state" means the state in which a child lived with a parent or a person acting as a parent for at least six consecutive months immediately before the commencement of a child custody proceeding. In the case of a child less than six months of age, the term means the state in which the child lived from birth with any of the persons mentioned. A period of temporary absence of any of the mentioned persons is part of the period.

"Initial determination" means the first child custody determination concerning a particular child.

"Issuing court" means the court that makes a child custody determination for which enforcement is sought under this act.

"Issuing state" means the state in which a child custody determination is made.

"Modification" means a child custody determination that changes, replaces, supersedes, or is otherwise made after a previous determination concerning the same child, whether or not it is made by the court that made the previous determination.

"Person" means an individual, corporation, business trust, estate, trust, partnership, limited liability company, association, joint venture, government, governmental subdivision, agency, or instrumentality, public corporation or any other legal or commercial entity.

"Person acting as a parent" means a person, other than a parent, who:

a. has physical custody of the child or has had physical custody for a period of six consecutive months, including any temporary absence, within one year immediately before the commencement of a child custody proceeding; and

b. has been awarded legal custody by a court or claims a right to legal custody under the laws of this State.

"Physical custody" means the physical care and supervision of a child.

"State" means a state of the United States, the District of Columbia, Puerto Rico, the United States Virgin Islands, or any territory or insular possession subject to the jurisdiction of the United States.

"Tribe" means an Indian tribe or band, or Alaskan Native village, which is recognized by federal law or formally acknowledged by a state.

"Warrant" means an order issued by a court authorizing law enforcement officers to take physical custody of a child.

L.2004,c.147,s.2.

2A:34-55 Proceedings governed by other law.

Proceedings Governed by Other Law.

This act does not govern an adoption proceeding or a proceeding pertaining to the authorization of emergency medical care for a child.

L.2004,c.147,s.3.

2A:34-56 Application to Indian tribes.

Application to Indian Tribes.

a. A child custody proceeding that pertains to an Indian child as defined in the Indian Child Welfare Act, 25 U.S.C.1901 et seq., is not subject to this act to the extent that it is governed by the Indian Child Welfare Act.

b. A court of this State shall treat a tribe as if it were a state of the United States for purposes of articles 1 and 2 of this act.

c. A child custody determination made by a tribe under factual circumstances in substantial conformity with the jurisdictional standards of this act shall be recognized and enforced under the provisions of article 3 of this act.

L.2004,c.147,s.4.

2A:34-57 International application of act.

International Application of Act.

a. A court of this State shall treat a foreign country as if it were a state of the United States for the purpose of applying articles 1 and 2 of this act if the foreign court gives notice and an opportunity to be heard to all parties before making child custody determinations.

b. A child custody determination made in a foreign country under factual circumstances in substantial conformity with the jurisdictional standards of this act shall be recognized and enforced under article 3 of this act.

c. A court of this State need not apply this act if the child custody law of a foreign country violates fundamental principles of human rights or does not base custody decisions on evaluation of the best interests of the child.

L.2004,c.147,s.5.

2A:34-58 Effect of custody determination.

Effect of Custody Determination.

A child custody determination made by a court of this State that had jurisdiction under this act binds all persons who have been served in accordance with the laws of this State or notified in accordance with section 8 of this act or who have submitted to the jurisdiction of the court, and who have been given an opportunity to be heard. As to those persons, the determination is conclusive as to all decided issues of law and fact except to the extent the determination is modified.

L.2004,c.147,s.6.

2A:34-59 Priority.

7. Priority.

If a question of existence or exercise of jurisdiction under this act is raised in a child custody proceeding, the question, upon request of a party, shall be given priority on the calendar and handled expeditiously.

L.2004,c.147,s.7.

2A:34-60 Notice of persons outside state.

8. Notice of Persons Outside State.

a. Notice required for the exercise of jurisdiction when a person is outside this State may be given in a manner prescribed by the law of this State for the service of process or by the law of the state in which the service is made. Notice shall be given in a manner reasonably calculated to give actual notice, but may be by publication if other means are not effective.

b. Proof of service may be made in the manner prescribed by the law of this State or by the law of the state in which the service is made.

c. Notice is not required for the exercise of jurisdiction with respect to a person who submits to the jurisdiction of the court. L.2004,c.147,s.8.

2A:34-61 *Appearance and limited immunity.*

9. Appearance and Limited Immunity.

a. A party to a child custody proceeding, including a modification proceeding, or a petitioner or a respondent in a proceeding to enforce or register a child custody determination, is not subject to personal jurisdiction in this State for another proceeding or purpose solely by reason of having participated, or of having been physically present for the purpose of participating in the proceeding.

b. A party who is subject to personal jurisdiction in this State on a basis other than physical presence is not immune from service of process in this State. A party present in this State who is subject to the jurisdiction of another state is not immune from service of process allowable under the laws of that state.

c. The immunity granted by subsection a. of this section does not extend to civil litigation based on acts unrelated to the participation in a proceeding under this act committed by an individual while present in this State.

L.2004,c.147,s.9.

2A:34-62 *Communication between courts.*

10. Communication Between Courts.

a. A court of this State may communicate with a court in another state concerning a proceeding arising under this act.

b. The court may allow the parties to participate in the communication. If the parties are not able to participate in the communication, the parties shall be given the opportunity to present facts and legal arguments before a decision on jurisdiction is made.

c. Communication between courts on schedules, calendars, court records and similar matters may occur without informing the parties. A record need not be made of that communication.

d. Except as provided in subsection c. of this section, a record shall be made of a communication under this section. The parties shall be informed promptly of the communication and granted access to the record.

e. For the purposes of this section, "record" means information that is inscribed on a tangible medium or that which is stored in an electronic or other medium and is retrievable in perceivable form. L.2004,c.147,s.10.

2A:34-63 Taking testimony in another state.

11. Taking Testimony in Another State.

a. In addition to other procedures available to a party, a party to a child custody proceeding may offer testimony of witnesses who are located in another state, including testimony of the parties and the child, by deposition or other means allowable in this State for testimony taken in another state. The court on its own motion may order that the testimony of a person be taken in another state and may prescribe the manner in which and the terms upon which the testimony is taken.

b. A court of this State may permit an individual residing in another state to be deposed or to testify by telephone, audiovisual means or other electronic means before a designated court or at another location in that state. A court of this State shall cooperate with courts of other states in designating an appropriate location for the deposition or testimony.

c. Documentary evidence transmitted from another state to a court of this State by technological means that do not produce an original writing may not be excluded from evidence on an objection based on the means of transmission. L.2004,c.147,s.11.

2A:34-64 Cooperation between courts; preservation of records.

12. Cooperation Between Courts; Preservation of Records.

a. A court of this State may request the appropriate court of another state to:

(1) hold an evidentiary hearing;

(2) order a person to produce or give evidence under procedures of that state;

(3) order that an evaluation be made with respect to the custody of a child involved in a pending proceeding;

(4) forward to the court of this State a certified copy of the transcript of the record of the hearing, the evidence otherwise presented, and any evaluation prepared in compliance with the request; and

(5) order a party to a child custody proceeding or any person having physical custody of the child to appear in the proceeding with or without the child.

b. Upon request of a court of another state, a court of this State may hold a hearing or enter an order described in subsection a. of this section.

c. Travel and other necessary and reasonable expenses incurred under subsections a. and b. of this section may be assessed against the parties according to the laws of this State.

d. A court of this State shall preserve the pleadings, orders, decrees, records of hearings, evaluations and other pertinent records with respect to a child custody proceeding until the child attains 18 years of age. Upon appropriate request by a court or law enforcement official of another state, the court shall forward a certified copy of these records.

L.2004,c.147,s.12.

2A:34-65 Initial child custody jurisdiction.

13. Initial Child Custody Jurisdiction.

a. Except as otherwise provided in section 16 of this act, a court of this State has jurisdiction to make an initial child custody determination only if:

(1) this State is the home state of the child on the date of the commencement of the proceeding, or was the home state of the child within six months before the commencement of the proceeding and the child is absent from this State but a parent or person acting as a parent continues to live in this State;

(2) a court of another state does not have jurisdiction under paragraph (1) of this subsection, or a court of the home state of the child has declined to exercise jurisdiction on the ground that this State is the more appropriate forum under section 19 or 20 of this act and:

(a) the child and the child's parents, or the child and at least one parent or a person acting as a parent have a significant connection with this State other than mere physical presence; and

(b) substantial evidence is available in this State concerning the child's care, protection, training and personal relationships;

(3) all courts having jurisdiction under paragraph (1) or (2) of this subsection have declined to exercise jurisdiction on the ground that a court of this State is the more appropriate forum to

determine the custody of the child under section 19 or 20 of this act; or

(4) no state would have jurisdiction under paragraph (1), (2) or (3) of this subsection.

b. Subsection a. of this section is the exclusive jurisdictional basis for making a child custody determination by a court of this State.

c. Physical presence of, or personal jurisdiction over, a party or a child is neither necessary nor sufficient to make a child custody determination.

d. A court of this State may assume temporary emergency jurisdiction in accordance with section 16 of this act.

L.2004,c.147,s.13.

2A:34-66 Exclusive, continuing jurisdiction.

14. Exclusive, Continuing Jurisdiction.

a. Except as otherwise provided in section 16 of this act, a court of this State that has made a child custody determination consistent with section 13 or 15 of this act has exclusive, continuing jurisdiction over the determination until:

(1) a court of this State determines that neither the child, the child and one parent, nor the child and a person acting as a parent have a significant connection with this State and that substantial evidence is no longer available in this State concerning the child's care, protection, training, and personal relationships; or

(2) a court of this State or a court of another state determines that neither the child, nor a parent, nor any person acting as a parent presently resides in this State.

b. A court of this State which has made a child custody determination and does not have exclusive, continuing jurisdiction under this section may modify that determination only if it has jurisdiction to make an initial determination under section 13 of this act.

L.2004,c.147,s.14.

2A:34-67 Jurisdiction to modify determination.

15. Jurisdiction to Modify Determination.

Except as otherwise provided in section 16 of this act, a court of this State may not modify a child custody determination made by a court of another state unless a court of this State has jurisdiction to make an initial determination under paragraph (1) or (2) of subsection a. of section 13 of this act and:

a. the court of the other state determines it no longer has exclusive, continuing jurisdiction under section 14 of this act or that a court of this State would be a more convenient forum under section 19 of this act; or

b. a court of this State or a court of the other state determines that the child, the child's parents, and any person acting as a parent do not presently reside in the other state.
L.2004,c.147,s.15.

2A:34-68 Temporary emergency jurisdiction.

16. Temporary Emergency Jurisdiction.

a. A court of this State has temporary emergency jurisdiction if the child is present in this State and the child has been abandoned or it is necessary in an emergency to protect the child because the child, or a sibling or parent of the child, is subjected to or threatened with mistreatment or abuse.

b. If there is no previous child custody determination that is entitled to be enforced under this act, and if no child custody proceeding has been commenced in a court of a state having jurisdiction under sections 13 through 15 of this act, a child custody determination made under this section remains in effect until an order is obtained from a court of a state having jurisdiction under sections 13 through 15 of this act. If a child custody proceeding has not been or is not commenced in a court of a state having jurisdiction under sections 13 through 15 of this act, a child custody determination made under this section becomes a final determination if:

(1) it so provides; and

(2) this State becomes the home state of the child.

c. If there is a previous child custody determination that is entitled to be enforced under this act, or a child custody proceeding has been commenced in a court of a state having jurisdiction under sections 13 through 15 of this act, any order issued by a court of this State under this section must specify in the order a period of time which the court considers adequate to allow the person seeking an order to obtain an order from the state having jurisdiction under sections 13 through 15 of this act. The order issued in this State remains in effect until an order is obtained from the other state within the period specified or the period expires.

d. A court of this State which has been asked to make a child custody determination under this section, upon being informed that a child custody proceeding has been commenced in, or a child custody determination has been made, by a court of a state having jurisdiction under sections 13 through 15 of this act, shall immediately communicate with the other court. A court of this State which is exercising jurisdiction pursuant to sections 13 through 15 of this act, upon being informed that a child custody proceeding has been commenced in, or a child custody determination has been made by, a court of another state under a statute similar to this section shall immediately communicate with the court of that state to resolve the emergency, protect the safety of the parties and the child, and determine a period for the duration of the temporary order.

L.2004,c.147,s.16.

2A:34-69 Notice; opportunity to be heard; joinder.

17. Notice; Opportunity to be Heard; Joinder.

a. Before a child custody determination is made under this act, notice and an opportunity to be heard in accordance with the standards of section 8 of this act shall be given to all persons entitled to notice under the law of this State as in child custody proceedings between residents of this State, any parent whose parental rights have not been previously terminated, and any person having physical custody of the child.

b. This act does not govern the enforceability of a child custody determination made without notice and an opportunity to be heard.

c. The obligation to join a party and the right to intervene as a party in a child custody proceeding under this act are governed by the law of this State as in child custody proceedings between residents of this State.

L.2004,c.147,s.17.

2A:34-70 Simultaneous proceedings.

18. Simultaneous Proceedings.

a. Except as otherwise provided in section 16 of this act, a court of this State may not exercise its jurisdiction under this article if at the time of the commencement of the proceeding a proceeding concerning the custody of the child had been commenced in a court of another state having jurisdiction substantially in conformity with this act, unless the proceeding has been terminated or is stayed by the court of the other state because a court of this State is a more convenient forum under section 19 of this act.

b. Except as otherwise provided in section 16 of this act, a court of this State, before hearing a child custody proceeding, shall examine the court documents and other information supplied by the parties pursuant to section 21 of this act. If the court determines that a child custody proceeding was previously commenced in a court in another state having jurisdiction substantially in accordance with this act, the court of this State shall stay its proceeding and communicate with the court of the other state. If the court of the state having jurisdiction substantially in accordance with this act does not determine that the court of this State is a more appropriate forum, the court of this State shall dismiss the proceeding.

c. In a proceeding to modify a child custody determination, a court of this State shall determine whether a proceeding to enforce the determination has been commenced in another state. If a proceeding to enforce a child custody determination has been commenced in another state, the court may:

(1) stay the proceeding for modification pending the entry of an order of a court of the other state enforcing, staying, denying or dismissing the proceeding for enforcement;

(2) enjoin the parties from continuing with the proceeding for enforcement; or

(3) proceed with the modification under conditions it considers appropriate.

L.2004,c.147,s.18.

2A:34-71 Inconvenient forum.

19. a. Inconvenient Forum.

A court of this State that has jurisdiction under this act to make a child custody determination may decline to exercise its jurisdiction at any time if it determines that it is an inconvenient forum under the circumstances and that a court of another state is a more appropriate forum. The issue of inconvenient forum may be raised upon the court's own motion, request of another court or motion of a party.

b. Before determining whether it is an inconvenient forum, a court of this State shall consider whether it is appropriate for a court of another state to exercise jurisdiction. For this purpose, the court shall allow the parties to submit information and shall consider all relevant factors, including:

(1) whether domestic violence has occurred and is likely to continue in the future and which state could best protect the parties and the child;

(2) the length of time the child has resided outside this State;

(3) the distance between the court in this State and the court in the state that would assume jurisdiction;

(4) the relative financial circumstances of the parties;

(5) any agreement of the parties as to which state should assume jurisdiction;

(6) the nature and location of the evidence required to resolve the pending litigation, including the testimony of the child;

(7) the ability of the court of each state to decide the issue expeditiously and the procedures necessary to present the evidence; and

(8) the familiarity of the court of each state with the facts and issues of the pending litigation.

c. If a court of this State determines that it is an inconvenient forum and that a court of another state is a more appropriate forum, it shall stay the proceedings upon condition that a child custody proceeding be promptly commenced in another designated state and may impose any other condition the court considers just and proper.

d. A court of this State may decline to exercise its jurisdiction under this act if a child custody determination is incidental to an action for divorce or another proceeding while still retaining jurisdiction over the divorce or other proceeding.

L.2004,c.147,s.19.

2A:34-72 Jurisdiction declined by reason of conduct.

20. Jurisdiction Declined by Reason of Conduct.

a. Except as otherwise provided in section 16 of this act or by other law of this State, if a court of this State has jurisdiction under this act because a person invoking the jurisdiction has engaged in unjustifiable conduct, the court shall decline to exercise its jurisdiction unless:

(1) the parents and all persons acting as parents have acquiesced in the exercise of jurisdiction;

(2) a court of the state otherwise having jurisdiction under sections 13 through 15 of this act determines that this State is a more appropriate forum under section 19 of this act; or

(3) no other State would have jurisdiction under sections 13 through 15 of this act.

b. If a court of this State declines to exercise its jurisdiction pursuant to subsection a. of this section, it may fashion an appropriate remedy to ensure the safety of the child and prevent a repetition of the wrongful conduct, including staying the proceeding until a child custody proceeding is commenced in a court having jurisdiction under sections 13 through 15 of this act.

c. If a court dismisses a petition or stays a proceeding because it declines to exercise its jurisdiction pursuant to subsection a. of this section, it shall charge the party invoking the jurisdiction of the court with necessary and reasonable expenses including costs, communication expenses, attorney's fees, investigative fees, expenses for witnesses, travel expenses, and child care during the course of the proceedings, unless the party from whom fees are sought establishes that the award would be inappropriate. The court may not assess fees, costs, or expenses against this State except as otherwise provided by law other than this act. No fees, costs or expenses shall be assessed against a party who is fleeing an incident or pattern of domestic violence or mistreatment or abuse of a child or sibling, unless the court is convinced by a preponderance of evidence that such assessment would be clearly appropriate.

d. In making a determination under this section, a court shall not consider as a factor weighing against the petitioner any taking of the child or retention of the child from the person who has rights of legal custody, physical custody or visitation, if there is evidence that the taking or retention of the child was to protect the petitioner from domestic violence or to protect the child or sibling from mistreatment or abuse.

L.2004,c.147,s.20.

2A:34-73 Information to be submitted to court.

21. Information to be Submitted to Court.

a. Unless a party seeks an exception to disclosure of information as provided by subsection e. of this section, each party, in its first pleading or in an attached affidavit, shall give information, if reasonably ascertainable, under oath as to the child's present address, the places where the child has lived during the last five years, and the names and present addresses of the persons with whom the child has lived during that period. The pleading or affidavit shall state whether the party:

(1) has participated, as a party or witness or in any other capacity, in any other proceeding concerning the custody of or visitation with the child and, if so, identify the court, the case number of the proceeding, and the date of the child custody determination, if any;

(2) knows of any proceeding that could affect the current proceeding, including proceedings for enforcement and proceedings relating to domestic violence, protective orders, termination of parental rights and adoptions and, if so, identify the court and the case number and the nature of the proceeding; and

(3) knows the names and addresses of any person not a party to the proceeding who has physical custody of the child or claims rights of legal custody or physical custody of, or visitation with, the child and, if so, the names and addresses of those persons.

b. If the information required by subsection a. of this section is not furnished, the court, upon its own motion or that of a party, may stay the proceeding until the information is furnished.

c. If the declaration as to any of the items described in subsection a. of this section is in the affirmative, the declarant shall give additional information under oath as required by the court. The court may examine the parties under oath as to details of the information furnished and other matters pertinent to the court's jurisdiction and the disposition of the case.

d. Each party has a continuing duty to inform the court of any proceeding in this or any other state that could affect the current proceeding.

e. If a party alleges in an affidavit or a pleading under oath that the health, safety, or liberty of a party or child would be put at risk by the disclosure of identifying information, that information shall be sealed and not disclosed to the other party or the public unless the court orders the disclosure to be made after a hearing in which the court takes into consideration the health, safety, or liberty of the party or child and determines that the disclosure is in the interest of justice.

L.2004,c.147,s.21.

2A:34-74 Appearance of parties and child.

22. Appearance of Parties and Child.

a. In a child custody proceeding in this State, the court may order a party to a child custody proceeding who is in this State to appear before the court in person with or without the child. The court may order any person who is in this State and who has physical custody or control of the child to appear physically with the child.

b. If a party to a child custody proceeding whose presence is desired by the court is outside this state, the court may order that a notice given pursuant to section 8 of this act include a statement directing the party to appear personally with or without the child and declaring that failure to appear may result in a decision adverse to the party.

c. The court may enter any orders necessary to ensure the safety of the child and of any person ordered to appear under this section.

d. If a party to a child custody proceeding who is outside this state is directed to appear under subsection b. of this section or desires to appear personally before the court with or without the child, the court may require another party to pay reasonable and necessary travel and other expenses of the party so appearing and of the child.

L.2004,c.147,s.22.

2A:34-75 Definitions.

23. Definitions.

As used in this article:

"Petitioner" means a person who seeks enforcement of a child custody determination or enforcement of an order for the return of the child under the Hague Convention on the Civil Aspects of International Child Abduction.

"Respondent" means a person against whom a proceeding has been commenced for enforcement of a child custody determination or enforcement of an order for return of a child

under the Hague Convention on the Civil Aspects of International Child Abduction.
L.2004,c.147,s.23.

2A:34-76 Enforcement under Hague Convention.

24. Enforcement Under Hague Convention.
Under this article, a court of this State may enforce an order for the return of a child made under the Hague Convention on the Civil Aspects of International Child Abduction as if it were a child custody determination.
L.2004,c.147,s.24.

2A:34-77 Duty to enforce.

25. Duty to Enforce.
a. A court of this State shall recognize and enforce a child custody determination of a court of another state if the latter court exercised jurisdiction in substantial conformity with this act or the determination was made under factual circumstances meeting the jurisdictional standards of this act and the determination has not been modified in accordance with this act.
b. A court of this State may utilize any remedy available under other law of this State to enforce a child custody determination made by a court of another state. The remedies provided in this article are cumulative and do not affect the availability of other remedies to enforce a child custody determination.
L.2004,c.147,s.25.

2A:34-78 Temporary visitation.

26. Temporary Visitation.
a. A court of this State which does not have jurisdiction to modify a child custody determination may issue a temporary order enforcing:
(1) a visitation schedule made by a court of another state; or
(2) the visitation provisions of a child custody determination of another state that does not provide for a specific visitation schedule.
b. If a court of this State makes an order under paragraph (2) of subsection a. of this section, it shall specify in the order a period that it considers adequate to allow the petitioner to obtain an order from a court having jurisdiction under the criteria specified

in article 2 of this act. The order remains in effect until an order is obtained from the other court or the period expires.
L.2004,c.147,s.26.

2A:34-79 Registration of child custody determination.

27. Registration of Child Custody Determination.

a. A child custody determination issued by a court of another state may be registered in this State, with or without a simultaneous request for enforcement, by sending to the Superior Court in this State:

(1) a letter or other document requesting registration;

(2) two copies, including one certified copy, of the determination sought to be registered, and a statement under penalty of perjury that to the best of the knowledge and belief of the person seeking registration the order has not been modified; and

(3) except as otherwise provided in section 21 of this act, the name and address of the person seeking registration and any parent or person acting as a parent who has been awarded custody or visitation in the child custody determination sought to be registered.

b. On receipt of the documents required by subsection a. of this section, the registering court shall:

(1) cause the determination to be filed as a foreign judgment, together with one copy of any accompanying documents and information, regardless of their form; and

(2) serve notice upon the persons named pursuant to paragraph (3) of subsection a. of this section and provide them with an opportunity to contest the registration in accordance with this section.

c. The notice required by paragraph (2) of subsection b. of this section shall state that:

(1) a registered determination is enforceable as of the date of the registration in the same manner as a determination issued by a court of this State;

(2) a hearing to contest the validity of the registered determination shall be requested within 20 days after service of notice; and

(3) failure to contest the registration will result in confirmation of the child custody determination and preclude further contest of that determination with respect to any matter that could have been asserted.

d. A person seeking to contest the validity of a registered order shall request a hearing within 20 days after service of the notice. At that hearing, the court shall confirm the registered order unless the person contesting registration establishes that:

(1) the issuing court did not have jurisdiction under article 2 of this act;

(2) the child custody determination sought to be registered has been vacated, stayed, or modified by a court of a state having jurisdiction to do so under article 2 of this act; or

(3) the person contesting registration was entitled to notice, but notice was not given in accordance with the standards of section 8 of this act in the proceedings before the court that issued the order for which registration is sought.

e. If a timely request for a hearing to contest the validity of the registration is not made, the registration is confirmed as a matter of law and the person requesting registration and all persons served must be notified of the confirmation.

f. Confirmation of a registered order, whether by operation of law or after notice and hearing, precludes further contest of the order with respect to any matter which could have been asserted at the time of registration.

L.2004,c.147,s.27.

2A:34-80 Enforcement of registered determination.

28. Enforcement of Registered Determination.

a. A court of this State may grant any relief normally available under the law of this State to enforce a registered child custody determination made by a court of another state.

b. A court of this State shall recognize and enforce, but may not modify, except in accordance with article 2 of this act, a registered child custody determination of another state.

L.2004,c.147,s.28.

2A:34-81 Simultaneous proceedings.

29. Simultaneous Proceedings.

If a proceeding for enforcement under this article has been or is commenced in a court of this State and the court determines that a proceeding to modify the determination is pending in a court of another state having jurisdiction to modify the determination under article 2 of this act, the enforcing court shall immediately communicate with the modifying court. The proceeding for enforcement continues unless the enforcing court, after consultation with the modifying court, stays or dismisses the proceeding.

L.2004,c.147,s.29.

2A:34-82 Expedited enforcement of child custody determination.

30. Expedited Enforcement of Child Custody Determination.

a. A petition under this article shall be verified. Certified copies of all orders sought to be enforced and of the order confirming registration, if any, shall be attached to the petition. A copy of a certified copy of an order may be attached instead of the original.

b. A petition for enforcement of a child custody determination shall state:

(1) whether the court that issued the determination identified the jurisdictional basis it relied upon in exercising jurisdiction and, if so, what the basis was;

(2) whether the determination for which enforcement is sought has been vacated, stayed, or modified by a court whose decision must be enforced under this act and, if so, identify the court, the case number, and the nature of the proceeding;

(3) whether any proceeding has been commenced that could affect the current proceeding, including proceedings relating to domestic violence, protective orders, termination of parental rights, and adoptions and, if so, identify the court and the case number and the nature of the proceeding;

(4) the present physical address of the child and the respondent, if known; and

(5) whether relief in addition to the immediate physical custody of the child and attorney's fees is sought, including a request for assistance from law enforcement officials and, if so, the relief sought: and

(6) if the child custody determination has been registered and confirmed under section 27 of this act, the date and place of registration.

c. Upon the filing of a petition, the court shall issue an order directing the respondent to appear in person with or without the child at a hearing and may enter any orders necessary to ensure the safety of the parties and the child. The hearing shall be held on the next judicial day following service of process unless that date is impossible. In that event, the court shall hold the hearing on the first day possible. The court may extend the date of hearing at the request of the petitioner.

d. An order issued under subsection c. of this section shall state the time and place of the hearing and advise the respondent that at the hearing the court will order that the petitioner may take immediate physical custody of the child and the payment of fees, costs, and expenses under section 34 of this act, and may schedule a hearing to determine whether further relief is appropriate, unless the respondent appears and establishes that:

(1) the child custody determination has not been registered and confirmed under section 27 of this act, and that

(a) the issuing court did not have jurisdiction under article 2 of this act;

(b) the child custody determination for which enforcement is sought has been vacated, stayed, or modified by a court of a state having jurisdiction to do so under article 2 of this act; or

(c) the respondent was entitled to notice, but notice was not given in accordance with the standards of section 8 in the proceedings before the court that issued the order for which enforcement is sought; or

(2) the child custody determination for which enforcement is sought was registered and confirmed under section 27 of this act, but has been vacated, stayed or modified by a court of a state having jurisdiction to do so under article 2 of this act or federal law.

L.2004,c.147,s.30.

2A:34-83 Service of petition and order.

31. Service of Petition and Order.

Except as otherwise provided in section 33 of this act, the petition and order shall be served, by any method authorized by the law of this State, upon the respondent and any person who has physical custody of the child.

L.2004,c.147,s.31.

2A:34-84 Hearing and order.

32. Hearing and Order.

a. Unless the court enters a temporary emergency order pursuant to section 16 of this act, upon a finding that a petitioner is entitled to the physical custody of the child immediately, the court shall order the child delivered to the petitioner unless the respondent establishes that:

(1) the child custody determination has not been registered and confirmed under section 27 of this act, and that

(a) the issuing court did not have jurisdiction under article 2 of this act;

(b) the child custody determination for which enforcement is sought has been vacated, stayed or modified by a court of a state having jurisdiction to do so under article 2 of this act or federal law; or

(c) the respondent was entitled to notice, but notice was not given in accordance with the standards of section 8 of this act in the proceedings before the court that issued the order for which enforcement is sought; or

(2) the child custody determination for which enforcement is sought was registered and confirmed under section 27 of this act, but has been vacated, stayed or modified by a court of a state having jurisdiction to do so under article 2 of this act or federal law.

b. The court shall award the fees, costs, and expenses authorized under section 34 of this act and may grant additional relief, including a request for the assistance of law enforcement officials, and set a further hearing to determine whether additional relief is appropriate.

c. If a party called to testify refuses to answer on the ground that the testimony may be self-incriminating, the court may draw an adverse inference from the refusal.

d. A privilege against disclosure of communications between spouses and a defense of immunity based on the relationship of husband and wife or parent and child may not be invoked in a proceeding under this article.

L.2004,c.147,s.32.

2A:34-85 Warrant to take physical custody of child.

33. Warrant to Take Physical Custody of Child.

a. Upon the filing of a petition seeking enforcement of a child custody determination, the petitioner may file a verified application for the issuance of a warrant to take physical custody of the child if the child is likely to suffer serious imminent physical harm or removal from this State.

b. If the court, upon the testimony of the petitioner or other witness, finds that the child is likely to suffer serious imminent physical harm or be imminently removed from this State, it may issue a warrant to take physical custody of the child. The petition shall be heard on the next judicial day after the warrant is executed. The warrant shall include the statements required by subsection b. of section 30 of this act.

c. A warrant to take physical custody of a child shall:

(1) recite the facts upon which a conclusion of serious imminent physical harm or removal from the jurisdiction is based;

(2) direct law enforcement officers to take physical custody of the child immediately;

(3) provide for the placement of the child pending final relief.

d. The respondent shall be served with the petition, warrant and order immediately after the child is taken into physical custody.

e. A warrant to take physical custody of a child is enforceable throughout this State. If the court finds on the basis of the testimony of the petitioner or other witness that a less intrusive remedy is not effective, it may authorize law enforcement officers to enter private property to take physical custody of the child. If required by the exigency of the case, the court may authorize law enforcement officers to make a forcible entry at any hour.

f. The court may impose conditions upon placement of a child to ensure the appearance of the child and the child's custodian. After the issuance of any temporary or permanent order determining custody or visitation of a minor child, a law enforcement officer having reasonable cause to believe that a person is likely to flee the State with the child or otherwise by flight or concealment evade the jurisdiction of the courts of this State may take a child into protective custody and return the child to the parent having lawful custody, or to a court in which a custody hearing concerning the child is pending.

g. After the issuance of any temporary or permanent order determining custody or visitation of a minor child, a law enforcement officer having reasonable cause to believe that a person is likely to flee the State with the child or otherwise by flight or concealment evade the jurisdiction of the courts of this State may take a child into protective custody and deliver the

child to a court in which a custody hearing concerning the child is pending.
L.2004,c.147,s.33.

2A:34-86 Costs, fees and expenses.

34. Costs, Fees and Expenses.
a. The court shall award the prevailing party, including a state, necessary and reasonable expenses incurred by or on behalf of the party, including costs, communication expenses, attorney's fees, investigative fees, expenses for witnesses, travel expenses, and child care during the course of the proceedings, unless the party from whom fees or expenses are sought establishes that the award would be clearly inappropriate.
b. The court may not assess fees, costs, or expenses against a state except as otherwise provided by law other than this act.
L.2004,c.147,s.34.

2A:34-87 Recognition and Enforcement.

35. Recognition and enforcement.
A court of this State shall accord full faith and credit to an order made consistently with this act which enforces a child custody determination by a court of another state unless the order has been vacated, stayed, or modified by a court authorized to do so under article 2 of this act.
L.2004,c.147,s.35.

2A:34-88 Appeals.

36. Appeals.
An appeal may be taken from a final order in a proceeding under this article in accordance with expedited appellate procedures in other civil cases. Unless the court enters a temporary emergency order under section 16 of this act, the enforcing court may not stay an order enforcing a child custody determination pending appeal.
L.2004,c.147,s.36.

2A:34-89 Role of prosecutor or other appropriate public official.

37. Role of Prosecutor or Other Appropriate Public Official.
a. In a case arising under this act or involving the Hague Convention on the Civil Aspects of International Child Abduction, the prosecutor or other appropriate public official may take any

lawful action, including resort to a proceeding under this article or any other available civil proceeding to locate a child, obtain the return of a child, or enforce a child custody determination if there is:

(1) an existing child custody determination;

(2) a request from a court in a pending child custody case;

(3) a reasonable belief that a criminal statute has been violated; or

(4) a reasonable belief that the child has been wrongfully removed or retained in violation of the Hague Convention on the Civil Aspects of International Child Abduction.

b. A prosecutor or other appropriate public official acts on behalf of the court and may not represent any party to a child custody determination.

L.2004,c.147,s.37.

2A:34-90 Role of law enforcement.

38. Role of Law Enforcement.

At the request of a prosecutor or other appropriate public official acting under section 37 of this act, a law enforcement officer may take any lawful action reasonably necessary to locate a child or a party and assist a prosecutor or other appropriate public official with responsibilities under section 37 of this act.

L.2004,c.147,s.38.

2A:34-91 Costs and expenses.

39. Costs and Expenses.

If the respondent is not the prevailing party, the court may assess against the respondent all direct expenses and costs incurred by the prosecutor or other appropriate public official and law enforcement officers under section 37 or 38 of this act.

L.2004,c.147,s.39.

2A:34-92 Application and construction.

40. Application and Construction.

In applying and construing this uniform act, consideration shall be given to the need to promote uniformity of the law with respect to its subject matter among states that enact it.

L.2004,c.147,s.40.

2A:34-93 Severability.

41. Severability.

If any provision of this act or its application to any person or circumstance is held invalid, the invalidity does not affect other provisions or applications of this act which can be given effect without the invalid provision or application, and to this end the provisions of this act are severable.
L.2004,c.147,s.41.

2A:34-94 Transitional provision.

42. Transitional Provision.
A motion or other request for relief made in a child custody or enforcement proceeding which was commenced before the effective date of this act is governed by the law in effect at the time the motion or other request was made.
L.2004,c.147,s.42.

2A:34-95 Notice of penalties for order violation.

43. Notice of Penalties for Order Violation.
Every order of a court involving custody or visitation shall include a written notice, in both English and Spanish, advising the persons affected as to the penalties provided in N.J.S.2C:13-4 for violating that order.
L.2004,c.147,s.43.

Uniform Premarital Agreement Act

Title 37, Chapter 2: Legal Rights and Liabilities; Contracts; Conveyances; Premarital Agreements

37:2-31. Short Title

This article shall be known and may be cited as the "Uniform Premarital Agreement Act." Source: New.
L. 1988, c. 99, s. 1.

37:2-32. Definitions

As used in this article:
a. "Premarital agreement" means an agreement between prospective spouses made in contemplation of marriage and to be effective upon marriage;
b. "Property" means an interest, present or future, legal or equitable, vested or contingent, in real or personal property, including income and earnings;

c. "Unconscionable premarital agreement" means an agreement, either due to a lack of property or unemployability:

(1) Which would render a spouse without a means of reasonable support;

(2) Which would make a spouse a public charge; or

(3) Which would provide a standard of living far below that which was enjoyed before the marriage. Source: New.

L. 1988, c. 99, s. 1.

37:2-33. Formalities; consideration

A premarital agreement shall be in writing, with a statement of assets annexed thereto, signed by both parties, and it is enforceable without consideration. Source: New.

L. 1988, c. 99, s. 1.

37:2-34. Contents of premarital agreement

Parties to a premarital agreement may contract with respect to:

a. The rights and obligations of each of the parties in any of the property of either or both of them whenever and wherever acquired or located;

b. The right to buy, sell, use, transfer, exchange, abandon, lease, consume, expend, assign, create a security interest in, mortgage, encumber, dispose of, or otherwise manage and control property;

c. The disposition of property upon separation, marital dissolution, death, or the occurrence or nonoccurrence of any other event;

d. The modification or elimination of spousal support;

e. The making of a will, trust, or other arrangement to carry out the provisions of the agreement;

f. The ownership rights in and disposition of the death benefit from a life insurance policy;

g. The choice of law governing the construction of the agreement; and

h. Any other matter, including their personal rights and obligations, not in violation of public policy. Source: New.

L. 1988, c. 99, s. 1.

37:2-35. Premarital agreement not to adversely affect right of child support

A premarital agreement shall not adversely affect the right of a child to support. Source: New.

L. 1988, c. 99, s. 1.

37:2-36. When premarital agreement becomes effective

A premarital agreement becomes effective upon marriage of the parties. Source: New.

L. 1988, c. 99, s. 1.

37:2-37. Amendment or revocation of premarital agreement

After marriage of the parties, a premarital agreement may be amended or revoked only by a written agreement signed by the parties, and the amended agreement or revocation is enforceable without consideration. Source: New.

L. 1988, c. 99, s. 1.

37:2-38. Enforcement of premarital agreement; generally

The burden of proof to set aside a premarital agreement shall be upon the party alleging the agreement to be unenforceable. A premarital agreement shall not be enforceable if the party seeking to set aside the agreement proves, by clear and convincing evidence, that:

a. The party executed the agreement involuntarily; or

b. The agreement was unconscionable at the time enforcement was sought; or

c. That party, before execution of the agreement:

(1) Was not provided full and fair disclosure of the earnings, property and financial obligations of the other party;

(2) Did not voluntarily and expressly waive, in writing, any right to disclosure of the property or financial obligations of the other party beyond the disclosure provided;

(3) Did not have, or reasonably could not have had, an adequate knowledge of the property or financial obligations of the other party; or

(4) Did not consult with independent legal counsel and did not voluntarily and expressly waive, in writing, the opportunity to consult with independent legal counsel.

d. The issue of unconscionability of a premarital agreement shall be determined by the court as a matter of law. Source: New.

L. 1988, c. 99, s. 1.

37:2-39. Enforcement of premarital agreement; marriage determined void

If a marriage is determined to be void, an agreement that would otherwise have been a premarital agreement is enforceable only to the extent necessary to avoid an inequitable result. Source: New.
L. 1988, c. 99, s. 1.

37:2-40. Construction of article

This article shall be construed to effectuate its general purpose to make uniform the law with respect to the subject of the article among states enacting the "Uniform Premarital Agreement Act." Source: New.
L. 1988, c. 99, s. 1.

37:2-41. Application of article

This article shall apply to premarital agreements executed on and after its effective date. Source: New.
L. 1988, c. 99, s. 1.

TABLE OF AUTHORITIES

CASES

STATUTES

CONSTITUTIONAL PROVISIONS

INDEX

A

abandonment, 19, 23, 26, 27, 76, 77, 86

abortion, 1, 5, 53, 54, 55, 56, 57, 58, 59
  Parental Notification for Abortion Act, 59
  partial-birth abortion, 56, 57, 58

adoption, 1, 3, 64, 66, 84, 85, 86, 87, 88, 89, 125, 128, 163, 166
  adoptive parents, 85, 86, 87, 88, 124
  open adoption, 89
  private adoption, 86, 87
  procedures, 86

adultery, 19, 22, 23, 24, 25, 28, 36, 39

alimony, 5, 18, 23, 33, 35, 36, 37, 38, 39, 40, 41, 42, 81, 82, 83
  modification, 40
  pendente lite alimony, 41, 42
  rehabilitative spousal support, 41
  tax consequences, 42
  termination, 39

annulment, 8, 10, 11, 12, 25, 41, 127, 130
  void marriage, 10
  voidable marriage, 11

artificial insemination, 65, 68, 129

assisted reproductive technology, 1, 65, 68

B

best interests of the child, 63, 69, 71, 72, 73, 74, 76, 77, 78, 85, 86, 87, 89, 135, 136, 138, 157, 167

bigamy, 8, 93

C

child support, 3, 4, 5, 22, 40, 42, 48, 61, 64, 71, 77, 81, 82, 83, 84, 94, 125, 136, 147, 162, 164, 189
  modification, 83
  termination, 84

commingling, 33, 34

common law marriage, 9, 10

community property, 31, 32, 35

competence, 8, 52, 76, 88, 105, 114, 125, 133

Comprehensive Child Abuse Prevention and Treatment Act, 51, 103

covenant marriage, 19

custody, 3, 22, 40, 48, 49, 52, 66, 69, 70, 71, 72, 73, 74, 75, 76, 77, 78, 81, 86, 103, 105, 135, 147, 149, 150, 154, 155, 156, 157, 160, 162, 164, 165, 166, 167, 168, 169, 170, 171, 172, 173, 174, 175, 176, 177, 178, 179, 180, 181, 182, 183, 184, 185, 186, 187, 188
  interference, 78
  modification, 77
  rights of sex-assault convicts, 77
  rights of third parties, 73, 75

termination, 76

D

Defense of Marriage Act, vii, 15, 16

divorce, 3, 8, 10, 12, 17, 18, 19, 21, 22, 23, 24, 25, 26, 27, 28, 29, 30, 31, 32, 34, 35, 36, 38, 41, 42, 50, 63, 67, 69, 70, 77, 81, 91, 96, 121, 127, 130, 164, 175

defenses to divorce, 27

divorce from bed and board, 23, 37, 41, 42, 50

divorce from the bonds of matrimony, 23

domestic partnership, vii, 12, 114, 115, 116, 117, 118, 119, 120, 121

domestic violence, 3, 45, 46, 47, 49, 139, 140, 141, 142, 143, 144, 145, 146, 147, 148, 149, 150, 151, 152, 153, 154, 155, 156, 159, 160, 162, 163, 164, 175, 176, 177, 182

due process, 21, 62, 91, 92, 93, 101

procedural due process, 91, 92

substantive due process, 91, 92

E

equal protection, 13, 14, 37, 59, 69, 91, 95, 96, 97, 101

equitable distribution, 31, 32, 34, 35, 36, 37, 38, 39, 40, 81, 82, 83, 122

G

guardian, 88, 113

guardian *ad litem*, 88

H

homosexual co-habitants, 88

homosexual rights advocates, 16

I

in vitro fertilization, 65, 67

incompetence. *See competence*

L

law enforcement, 46, 107, 108, 113, 114, 140, 141, 142, 143, 144, 145, 146, 147, 148, 153, 155, 157, 158, 160, 161, 163, 166, 170, 182, 184, 185, 187

M

marital contract, 17, 22

postnuptial agreements, 19

premarital agreements, 17, 191

marital privileges, 50

marital property, 31, 32, 33, 34, 35, 37, 38, 83

marriage, 1, 3, 7, 8, 9, 10, 11, 12, 13, 14, 15, 16, 17, 18, 19, 21, 23, 26, 28, 29, 31, 32, 33, 34, 35, 36, 37, 38, 43, 50, 63, 65, 91, 94, 95, 116, 118, 123, 127, 148, 149, 188, 189, 190, 191

mediation, 30, 155

Mediation, 30

N

New Jersey Parentage Act, 61, 64, 124

www.ingramcontent.com/pod-product-compliance
Lightning Source LLC
Chambersburg PA
CBHW021557210326
41599CB00010B/486